THE OFF SWITCH

Anna Charles

For Boy.

Acknowledgements

This book would not have been possible without the support and contribution of two brilliant people:

Boy - the genius behind the Off Switch app who patiently answered all my tech questions.

Evie Mannion - for your utterly fabulous illustrations. You're a talented animator who will go far! Thank you!

Foreword

This is not another book about abstinence. I'm not going to tell you that sobriety is best, or that alcohol is poison - only that trusting yourself around wine is the biggest buzz.

I'm not a doctor, nor am I a therapist, but I do have excellent credentials to write this book. For years I was an expert white wine drinker, majoring in French Chablis. I know what it's like to be confused by drinking. For it to be the one area in life where you lack control.

I wasn't what you'd call 'a drinker.' My family wasn't known for heavy boozing and I didn't hang out with a wild crowd. For three decades I was a high achieving corporate girl, thriving at Fortune 500 companies. But as I took on leadership roles with greater responsibility and stress, my drinking habits subtly changed. Alcohol sneaked up on me. A chilled glass of white became my go-to reward at the end of a long day.

To most observers, my drinking appeared social and moderate. I never developed a physical dependency. I didn't black out. Nor did I hit any kind of rock bottom. But I did find myself drinking more than I wanted to. It was frustrating. And absurd. I was a focused, determined go-getter. I was used to nailing goals. I'd done some pretty challenging things, but I couldn't drink one glass of wine and leave it at that? What was happening?

Something had to change. And that thing was me. So I decided to tackle my drinking as I would any other project: establish a hypothesis, apply it, evaluate progress, tweak as needed and repeat until successful.

I started by getting clear on my goal. That bit was easy: to have a take-it-or-leave-it relationship with dry white wine. But as for the action I'd been taking, that was a mess. I was embarrassed to see that my 'strategy' (such as it was) had relied on a mix of willpower (which always ran out) and hope… But as a wise CEO once told me, "Hope is not a strategy." It was time for an utterly different approach.

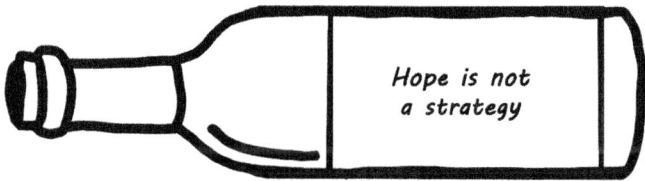

Hope is not a strategy

I recognised early on that I faced a skills gap, not some behavioural failing. I needed information, not recrimination. So I began learning about the brain, human behaviour and habit formation. I started imagining a different future. I wondered what it would be like to never even *think* about white wine. I started to daydream how that could make my life *way better*, even when that seemed impossible. And I committed to sorting this out, whatever it took. I knew that I was going to find a solution to this struggle, even though I had no idea how that would look. I trusted myself to stick at it, no matter the timeline.

My approach was 100% pragmatic, the result 100% miraculous. I started taking intentional, consistent action. I learned what worked, adapted as needed and kept going.

Within a few short months, my relationship with alcohol had done a complete 180.

I achieved this transformation without relying on gimmicks, medication, or recovery programs. The process was simple and I've maintained this take-it-or-leave-it relationship with alcohol for years. I understand why I don't feel the need to drink anymore so I'm confident I won't revert to old habits. Plus I feel secure that I have the necessary tools to maintain this new way of life. To call it liberating is an understatement.

I don't label myself sober, but I rarely drink because my desire for alcohol has vanished. Cravings and triggers, even for my once-loved French Chablis, have gone. Being around alcohol is now effortless.

The insights I gained were so profound that they prompted a career change. I left the corporate world to become a coach. I now help people to create a relationship with alcohol that works for them. This may mean drinking less, drinking now and then, or not drinking at all. I love working one-on-one with clients or in small groups, but what I've learned about drinking has been so transformative that I want to share it with as many people as possible. So I wrote this book.

Disclaimer

This book isn't part of a sober recovery program. It doesn't provide medical diagnosis or alcohol, drug addiction or substance abuse treatment, detoxification, or recovery services. It's not written for people who need alcohol to function, or who drink to avoid physical withdrawal symptoms. If you experience tremors, shakes, sweats, or feel physically ill without alcohol, please seek medical support. It's dangerous to just stop drinking without being under medical supervision.

Introduction

Want to strike it rich on the stock market? The recipe is simple: buy low, sell high. Rinse and repeat, and voilà – you're on your way to your very own private island! But how do you pick what to buy? Alas, that takes years of experience, a mountain of knowledge and maybe a dash of luck. Simple doesn't mean easy.

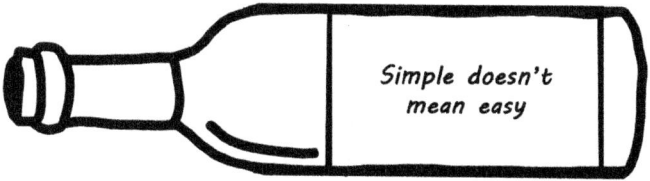

Simple doesn't mean easy

Whatever your goal, whether you're aiming to master the stock market, become fluent in a new language, or write the next bestseller, there's a cost involved. Even lottery winners have to buy a ticket! Changing your relationship with alcohol is no different. There's no secret spell or instant fix, just as there's no foolproof way to spot the next big stock. It's not always easy. It can feel downright hard at times. But it is simple. And doable. And so worth it.

Success at anything requires a full understanding of the task at hand and a willingness to do the work with focus, effort and discipline. We know this, yet still find ourselves clicking on 'sure-fire hacks' and searching for that one elusive *easy* solution to our problems. As a former colleague once told me, "The human capacity to ignore inconvenient facts and avoid unpleasantness is immense."

So, how do you drink less? Simple: put the glass down.

How do you do that? Read this book.

About This Book

Think of this book as your friendly guide, not as a rigid set of rules. I'm not here to dictate your goals - that's entirely up to you. Whether you want to learn how to wind down without wine, never drink home alone, give up alcohol altogether, or something else entirely, this book is here to support you. It will help you find a healthier relationship with alcohol that works for *you*. Think of it as a choose-your-own-adventure book, but instead of fighting dragons, you're mastering cravings.

This book doesn't use scare tactics, demonise alcohol, or preach abstinence. The aim is to give you control over your drinking as quickly and effectively as possible. It will show you how to cope with triggers and temptation without feeling deprived or miserable. It will show you how to make alcohol an irrelevance whether you continue to drink or not. And it will show you how to stop once you start - by means of your very own Off Switch - even if that sounds impossible right now.

This book is also short. It will only take you a couple of hours to read - so no excuses! It's also easy to flip back and re-read sections anytime you need a refresher.

About You

This book is written for smart, motivated high achievers who think they drink a bit too much; who realise that drinking is giving them a result they don't want; and who want to solve this struggle for once and for all without having to declare themselves broken or powerless. I don't believe you are helpless. I believe you have everything you need to demonstrate conscious control to yourself.

Whether you've been drinking too much for decades or have only recently noticed your recycling bin filling up faster than before, this book is for you. I'll assume you're a rational adult working on a behavioural challenge, not a hopeless addict. But this is not a 'do-this-one-thing-and-you're-healed' hack. It will take work. It will involve replacing immediate gratification with what you really want. The hard part is change - we don't like change. It's uncomfortable ... but so is living the same Ground Hog-style struggle day after day after day.

The effort is so worth it. When you learn how to build and operate your own Off Switch, you'll be able to decide how much you want to drink and trust yourself to drink just that. You'll feel powerful, proud and in control. You'll enjoy being you again - because when you transform your relationship with alcohol, you transform your relationship with yourself.

Once you've experienced this level of self-belief and self-trust, you won't go back to your old ways. No matter how much you used to believe that steak wouldn't taste as good without a glass of Cabernet Sauvignon.

About Your Reason Why

Let's start by asking why you're reading this book? And why you want to change your relationship with alcohol? Understanding your motivation for change is vital. It's what will carry you through the tough times. The three main reasons I hear time and again are:

Live Longer

This is often reason numero uno. Our livers weren't designed to handle decades of heavy drinking. Drinking less will make you healthier. Whatever you value in life, you can't enjoy it if you're dead. Consider the trade-off between a few uncomfortable days managing cravings or a few months of low-level irritation as you learn new skills, versus living ten years longer. Or seeing your children grow up. Or getting the money out of the pension you've been saving for decades. Whatever it is you're seeking in life, death prevents it all. Learning to change your relationship with alcohol might be no picnic. Some days may feel tough, but dropping dead is worse.

Better Health

Even if drinking too much doesn't shorten your life, by drinking too much you're far more likely to suffer health problems that will make life less enjoyable. Consider the physical symptoms of bloating, dull skin, poor memory, disturbed sleep, anxiety and frustration that you cannot control yourself. You can get accustomed to almost anything. If you've been drinking too much for a long time, it's hard to know what it's costing you. The only way to find out how great you'll feel without the daily drinks is to go through the process of implementing your Off Switch and experience the difference yourself.

Accomplish More

Drinking too much doesn't just damage your health, it prevents you from maximising what you do with your life.

Do you want to drink through a mediocre event or find one that's worth going to? Think about all the promotions you could get, the books you could read, the time you could spend being present with your family. It's all there for the taking when you stop frittering that time away drinking (and recovering). Implement your Off Switch and discover what you've been put on this world to accomplish.

Rewrite the 'Rules'

This starts with you deciding just what kind of relationship you want with alcohol. This is a personal decision and there's no right answer, even though society (and maybe your friends, spouse or complete strangers) may think otherwise.

When you attend a football match, supporters of the teams are separated - red and white at one end, blue and white at the other. If you've no allegiance to either team, you still have to sit somewhere. Even though you're neither for nor against either side, you're effectively forced to choose.

Enter the world of alcohol and it can feel the same. Are you on Team Drinking or Team Sober? It doesn't matter what you really want, you're told you have to choose. There's little middle ground. It's all or nothing. And it's nuts.

Imagine in my corporate life if I'd told my boss or customers: "You can have this or you can have that - decide!" I doubt I'd have stayed employed long or our business would have survived. But if you even *hint* to anyone that you think you drink a little too much, you'll be referred to AA or hushed by assurances of, "Stop making a fuss, you drink less than me!" No wonder people in the middle just keep quiet. You fear no one will understand.

I take a different approach. I talk about this openly. I trust you to know what's best for you. And I give you the tools to get what you want. Welcome to my label-free, judgment-free world.

A Few Final Words Before We Get Started

I know what you're going through. I know why you're afraid. Why you're worried this may not work for you. How it feels to have failed many times.

But I also know what it's like to succeed. How it feels to change. What it's like to see yourself in a whole new light, day after day after day. No wonder my clients say that working with me was, "The best money I ever spent." So stay with me. It may feel insurmountable today but just ask yourself: a year from now will you be glad you did this?

The sooner you're over this struggle, the sooner you can create a life that's focused on what you really want - instead of a life focused on whether there's enough wine in the fridge to last the week.

CHAPTER ONE

The Off Switch

A few years ago, I worked with a client I'll call Sarah. She was smart, successful, and the kind of person who looked like she had it all together - until she didn't. On the outside, she seemed unstoppable, but on the inside? Let's just say the wheels were coming off. Sarah had been in AA for years. She knew the drill - meetings, sharing her story, waiting to hit rock bottom. But deep down, she felt stuck. How did she see herself? "I'll always be an

addict. This is just who I am."

It wasn't that Sarah hated AA. She liked the coffee and the company. But over time, the label of 'hopeless addict' started to feel like wearing a name tag that said, Hi, I'm Broken! It wasn't exactly helping her believe she could be something different. She told me it felt as though the idea of being powerless over alcohol had unpacked its bags and made itself at home in every corner of her life. And that was making her wonder: could she really change, or was she destined to feel stuck forever?

Then, one day, a tiny, rebellious thought popped into her head: what if this isn't the whole story?

Now, this wasn't some Hollywood moment where Sarah threw open the curtains and declared, "Today is the first day of the rest of my life!" Nope. It was more of a quiet nudge. What else might be true? Maybe she didn't have to be sober forever. Maybe she wasn't doomed to spend the rest of her life dodging happy hour. Maybe - just maybe - there was a middle ground, a way to create her own path forward. Even though she had no idea how that might look.

That's when Sarah reached out to me. She didn't come in guns blazing with declarations about never drinking again. Instead, she said something simple: "I just want to stop feeling like alcohol runs the show."

That small change - from feeling trapped and hopeless to wondering what might be possible - was the catalyst for changing how Sarah saw herself and what she was truly capable of.

I like to reflect on clients like Sarah because it serves as a reminder that we each create our own reality. And here's the thing: Sarah's story isn't unusual. I've seen this play out time and again. When we stop seeing what's possible, we stop taking action. But the reverse is also true. *When we start*

rejecting the stories that keep us small - when we let ourselves dream a different life - that's when we begin to create a new reality.

So that's where we'll start - with what's possible. I want you to imagine you could have a way to control your drinking just like you control your heating. You would program the system by deciding when and how much you want to drink, then just get on with your life. When you reached your preset limit, the Off Switch would kick in.

Let's say you decide to have two glasses of wine on a date night. You program your Off Switch accordingly and after the second drink, the Off Switch will light up telling you to STOP. Or maybe you're enjoying a quiet night in and decide to be alcohol free. When the evening arrives, the Off Switch is lit: STOP.

You're the one who decides what to do. You can ignore the instruction if you wish. But by respecting your Off Switch you'll never drink too much. You would have complete control and trust yourself around alcohol. Problem solved. You'd be like one of those annoying people who always do the smart thing without any fuss or bother.

Now that's all very well, you might be thinking, but I don't have an Off Switch. Maybe so. But this doesn't mean you're condemned to endless drinking any more than a deaf person is to lifelong silence. You might not be able to buy an Off Switch as easily as a hearing aid, but you have a brain. You can create an Off Switch that does everything described - there's even an app to help! The Off Switch you'll discover in this book is simple to build, easy to use and highly effective in permanently controlling your drinking.

Lack of Feedback

I used to think how great it would be if I could drink alcohol in the same way I eat bananas. One banana makes a tasty snack. If I'm very hungry, I could manage two. But give me a bunch and it would be easy to say no. I'm very confident in my ability to control my banana intake because I know when I've had enough.

Alcohol is very different. In fact, when we drink, we go bananas! I don't mean literally of course, but it can feel as though that first glass puts us into drinking mode. We get used to 'checking out' and only coming back online when our glass is empty and it's time to decide whether we want more. If we pour another, we check out again until that glass is finished, and so on. No wonder we can consume so much alcohol without much thought. We're sitting there on the super highway consuming without hindrance. Overdrinking is swift, polished behaviour.

But imagine if you could drink wine the way I eat bananas. One glass: yes please. Two: maybe. Three or more: why? You'd be aware of every sip, you'd know when you'd had enough. This feedback would make all the difference.

I believe the main reason so many people struggle to control their drinking - even though they have the rest of their lives together - is because they lack this feedback. We have lost the ability to hear "enough already," but that's not a problem. Once upon a time if you were deaf you'd have to live with that impairment. Today, technology means you're no more disabled than the next person. So it is with the Off Switch. I'm going to teach you how to make an Off Switch that makes you as drink-proof as you are banana-proof. We're also going to do it without relying on willpower.

Why Willpower Doesn't Work

Yup, without willpower. Talk to anyone about cutting back or quitting alcohol, and you won't have to wait long until willpower enters the picture. So let's address that right away.

You don't need it to change your relationship with alcohol. I will say that again. You do not need willpower to change your relationship with alcohol.

Willpower is a finite resource, not a character trait. I think of willpower like a water bottle on a hike. It starts full, but the more you drink from it, the less water you have. By day's end you may have none left. And so it is with willpower.

We use up willpower in hundreds of little decisions all day long. Get up now or stay in bed? Go for a run or delay until tomorrow? Reply to this email now or do it later? Tell your boss what you really think of his idea or bite your tongue? On and on and on it goes. By 6pm we're exhausted. Our willpower is all used up. No wonder we give in and pour the wine. The moment we need willpower the most (the evenings) is the moment we have the least available. So we won't rely on it at all.

This book will help you to find motivation to change in the only place it can be found - within yourself - by laying out a program that makes the steps to success easy and the thought of backsliding difficult to contemplate. The goal is empowerment - the realisation, "Actually this isn't hard at all!" (something my private clients tell me all the time). It is such discoveries that give us the confidence and courage to go onward to greater challenges. The course of a life is often determined by such milestones and empowerment. When you change your relationship with alcohol you will change your life in more ways than you could possibly imagine.

Latent within you is the power to control your drinking for the rest of your life. All you need to do is realise that your drinking is under your conscious control. With this knowledge, and using your Off Switch, you'll be in a position to make this central to your self-image.

If you want to keep alcohol in your life, the stark reality is that this requires permanent attention to what you drink. Life long permanent attention. Just as permanent weight control requires permanent attention to what you eat. There is an all-too-human tendency to deny this simple fact. But like most unpleasant facts, it's best faced head-on and treated as a challenge to overcome.

The Success Formula

Successfully completing any project requires three key elements: a clear plan, the willingness to take action and consistently evaluating and learning from your results until you reach your goal. No plan: nothing. A plan without willingness to act: pointless. Action without evaluation: worthless.

Traditional approaches to drinking less fail because they lack one or more of these elements. They focus on getting you to just say "no" to effect a quick fix (no plan). They tell you to avoid temptation and distract yourself (no long-term viability). And they insist you go back to day one and just try harder whenever you give in and drink (no evaluation).

My approach is simple: plan how much you're going to drink; be willing to follow the plan by embracing the inevitable cravings; evaluate and learn from your results. Then repeat. This constitutes the Off Switch.

The Off Switch: How It Works

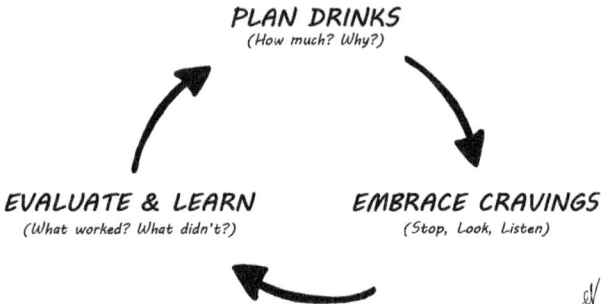

PLAN DRINKS
(How much? Why?)

EVALUATE & LEARN
(What worked? What didn't?)

EMBRACE CRAVINGS
(Stop, Look, Listen)

In the following chapters I'll show you, step-by-step, how to create and use your own Off Switch. You'll understand how and why it works, giving you complete confidence, founded on knowledge, that your drinking is totally and permanently under your control - no matter who you're with, what you're going through, or how you feel. You'll experience the sense of relief that comes from not only knowing *how* to do this, but in trusting yourself *to actually do it.* You'll go from worrying that you're one of those people who is destined to drink too much, to becoming someone who never does.

CHAPTER TWO

Why We Act the Way We Do

I write fiction in my spare time. After publishing a novel, I'm now diving into the world of screenwriting. My latest project is an action-adventure screenplay, complete with a nail-biting kidnap scene. Picture this: a beloved wife and mother gets snatched from the street in broad daylight. It's dramatic, it's intense, and to make it work as a Hollywood blockbuster, I know the scene needs to deliver all the tension - heart-pounding uncertainty, edge-of-your-

seat suspense and that relentless question: what's going to happen next?

But imagine if I made a total hash of it. Picture this alternative version.

The kidnapper calls the family, his voice low and menacing: "$1 million cash by 10 p.m., or you'll never see her again. Do not call the police."

And then - get this - the husband responds, "Hmm. You know, I'm swamped today. Back-to-back meetings. I'm exhausted. Can we maybe reschedule this? Tomorrow's looking a bit better for me."

Ridiculous, right? That's not how this works! A husband in this situation wouldn't shrug and check his calendar. He'd be panicked, laser-focused, and completely consumed by one thought: Save her.

What drives him to act so intensely, even if he doesn't have a clear plan? It's not just love - it's desire. Desire to rescue his wife from danger.

True desire overrides doubt, fear, and uncertainty. It becomes a single, unshakable focus, pushing you to take action even when you're way out of your depth. But here's the thing: desire doesn't just happen - it's part of how we're wired. When you understand how desire works, you can predict how it will drive you, how it might derail you, and how to steer it in the direction you want.

But what has this got to do with reducing the amount you drink? Just like writing a screenplay becomes easier when you understand how the system works - what creates tension, what keeps the audience hooked - reducing how much you drink becomes easier when you understand how *your* system works. The first step? Identifying what you want to control.

You might think the goal is to control the amount you drink, but we need to go deeper. *Why* do you drink? Do you know? I've heard hundreds of answers to this question, but they all boil down to one thing: we drink because we want to, because we desire it. That's it. Simple.

Think about it - if you didn't *want* the wine, beer, or champagne, you wouldn't drink it. In fact, I bet you're already doing this. I never drank whisky, for instance, because I never wanted it. And it was effortless not to. I'm sure there's something you wouldn't drink, even if it were the only option available.

So here's the truth: you don't just drink. You drink because you *want* to. So let's start by examining desire.

Desire Comes From Our Thoughts

Many people believe that desire is innate, that we have no choice over how we feel. How else to explain why I would feel a surge of desire for white wine every evening at 6pm when I logically *knew* I didn't want the drink?

Contrary to what we are often told, desire does not come from outside circumstances (people, places, things). It's 100% an inside job. Because desire, like *all* our emotions, is created by our thoughts. Even simple ones can be powerful. Consider: "I want it","I like it" or (my personal favourite) "I deserve it." These seemingly innocent thoughts can have you reaching for the corkscrew before you realise what you're doing. No wonder it can feel as though you don't control your desires.

This works for everything in life. Take ice cream, for example. I never have to hold myself back from it because it's not something I desire. You, on the other hand, may adore mint choc chip and find it impossible to put your spoon down. But ice cream is just chilled cream with flavourings; it's not inherently tasty or disgusting. How we act around it depends on what we think about it.

What else does desire impact? So many things. Your choice of car. Where you live. Who you date. Whether you drink or not. Take a bottle of Chablis - once my tipple of choice. Compare thinking, "I'd love a crisp glass of white - it's nectar" to, "White wine is disgusting." On a scale of 1 to 10, how likely are you to drink in these two situations? The difference is obvious, even though the wine in both cases is the *same*. This realisation is powerful because how you think about things is within your total control. *Always*.

So if you want to change your relationship with alcohol, you need to *start by thinking about it differently*. Whether you want to have a drink from time to time or cut it out completely, you make this manageable by liking and wanting it less.

Imagine looking at a glass of wine as though you were looking at a cup of wood. Yes, I realise that sounds a little weird but stay with me. You'd have zero desire for the cup of wood, right? You wouldn't be thinking how much you want it. So the million-dollar question is *do you want to want alcohol*? Pay deep attention to this. Your answer will influence every action you take and the speed with which you change.

For those of you saying, "I don't want it, but I just like it," do yourself a favour and stop insisting how much you love wine. Instead get curious. How much time and energy would the future version of you devote to thinking about alcohol?

Then ask what would they be dreaming about instead? Whatever it is, start today.

Practice and Repetition

We don't just desire alcohol by thinking about it. We teach ourselves to want it through practice and repetition, the only way humans ever learn anything. Our brains love to be efficient. When we repeat something, the brain recognises this as a pattern and creates an automatic program for it. Repeat this often enough and it becomes a habit - something that doesn't require much, if any, conscious thought.

We have hundreds of habits in our lives and many of them are positive. We clean our teeth twice a day without thinking about it. We know the route home so well that it feels second nature. Once upon a time these actions took conscious effort, but with practice they became automatic. It's the same with desire. Practice it enough and it becomes habitual behaviour.

Desire is not illogical or involuntary (though it can feel that way). Desire is something you learn and repeat. As you taught yourself to desire alcohol, you can also teach yourself something different (like *un*desiring it). Yes, even if this feels impossible right now.

Reward Reinforces Desire

If desire is just a practiced, repeated feeling created by your thoughts, why is it easier to develop a habit around drinking than, say, daily journalling? It comes down to the reward associated with the activity. Rewards reinforce habits. They help you memorise the behaviour.

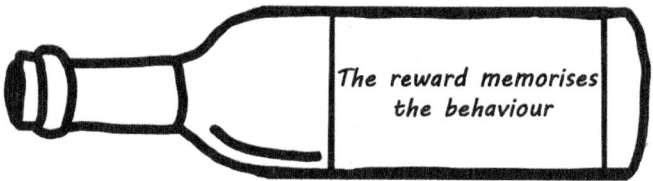

The reward memorises the behaviour

The more powerful the reward, the more quickly your brain will want to repeat that action. The reward in question is dopamine - a neurotransmitter released by the brain during enjoyable activities. What does that mean in simple terms? Dopamine plays a role in how we feel pleasure. Humans derive pleasure in all sorts of ways: in chatting with friends, eating, looking at flowers, feeling the sun on your face, achieving goals. Anything that gives us so much as a subtle dopamine response is going to trigger desire in us.

Alcohol gives a *super intense* level of dopamine. As this feels like such a huge reward to the brain, it will quickly want to experience this again - which is why you'll find it easier to get into the habit of drinking than, say, journalling.

This doesn't mean you're broken. It doesn't mean you're powerless, weak or out of control. It doesn't mean you can't change. It just means your brain is working as designed. Certain times, places, people, or situations serve as triggers - cues for all the conditions when you've taught your brain to *desire* and *expect* a drink. If you always share a bottle of wine with Janet after work on Fridays, this will become part of your brain's subconscious routine - even when you decide to take a break from drinking.

We feel ashamed and tormented by our lack of control, but I want you to put aside all judgment and see habits as *neutral*. Washing your face is a habit. Drinking a morning mug of tea is a habit. Calling your other-half "dear" is a habit. And you likely have no problems with any of these. Whether we see habits as 'good' or 'bad' depends on how we think about them.

Your Prefrontal Cortex Versus Your Lizard Brain

So why do you feel conflicted and continue to desire alcohol after you've decided to cut back? This comes down to how the different areas of your brain operate.

The prefrontal cortex is the rational piece that has your best interests at heart. It's good at planning and making decisions for the long-term. It's the area of your brain that decides to insert some alcohol free days into your week, that plans an early morning run, that wants you to get a good night's sleep.

However, your prefrontal cortex is not so hot at making quick decisions in the moment. That's the domain of your 'lizard' brain, the part that evaluates every moment of every day as a fight for survival. When faced with a mugger on a dark night, you want your lizard brain to take over and save you, but you don't want it in charge when there's a drink on offer. Your lizard brain is not interested in what you really want from life. It doesn't think logically. It only thinks about the here and now, about seeking pleasure and avoiding pain as efficiently as possible, just as it has for thousands of years of evolution. A lizard brain faced with a complimentary glass of champagne is like a toddler being asked if they'd like candy for dinner. Your lizard brain requires supervision.

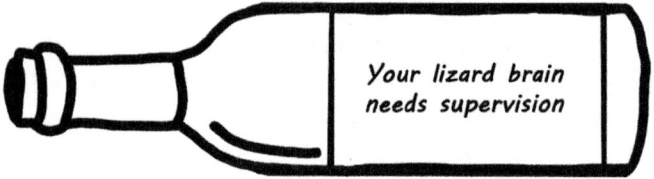

If you feel out of control around alcohol it means your lizard brain is currently in charge, making decisions in the moment when your desire is strong. That's all. But the good news is you are never actually out of control because you have a prefrontal cortex. You can use it to make different decisions and I'm going to teach you how.

Be warned! When you decide to use your prefrontal cortex in this way, your lizard brain will not be happy. It won't see the point of the change. It won't care that drinking is getting in the way of your bigger life plans. Its goal is to motivate you to continue drinking and seeking the reward (the 'buzz'). It does this by way of cravings.

What Are Cravings and Why Do We Feel Them?

A craving is simply an instruction to take immediate, urgent action. It consists of two parts: thoughts in our mind and sensations in our body. As we saw above, our thoughts always precede our feelings, even if we're not consciously aware of them. Thoughts such as "I'd love a drink" or "I deserve it," create the feelings of desire that have us reaching for a glass, often before we realise what we're doing.

But *without the thought that creates the desire, you won't feel the craving and you won't seek the drink*. So cravings aren't "terrible," "horrendous," "impossible," or "never-ending." They're simply intense *feelings* of desire created by thoughts designed to motivate you to take action.

Understanding your cravings is key to helping you figure out *why* you drink. There's always more beneath the drinking story, whether you drink to escape an emotion that you have but don't want (such as stress), or because you are seeking an emotion that you want but don't have (such as joy). So the shy executive at a client reception may drink to feel confident; the stressed project manager may drink to switch off at home; the lonely retiree may drink to alleviate boredom.

Ultimately, we drink to feel good. But we don't always feel good in life and that's okay. Stuff happens. There will be times when you lack confidence, feel stressed or bored. That's not a problem, because your feelings are never a problem. They are not beyond you and they don't need numbing with alcohol. Humans are built to handle emotions but taught how to bury them.

Habit change is the process of changing how you respond to your feelings in a way that serves you. When you do this, cravings lose their power. I'll show you how to wield that power in chapter five.

CHAPTER THREE

Feedback

It was a Friday night. I was dining at Mario's Pizzeria with friends, trying to strike that perfect balance - enough wine to feel relaxed, but not so much that I'd cross into the "you're embarrassing yourself" zone.

I'd had a couple of glasses of Verdicchio (when in Rome…), and at first everything felt fine. But then the self-doubt crept in. Am I talking too much? I thought. Why am I laughing so loudly? I glanced around the table. Was I the only one finding everything hilarious?

I looked down at my glass. Had I been drinking faster than the others? It felt so, but maybe I was just overthinking it. I didn't want to be that person who gets ahead of the group, so I slowed down, took a longer sip, and tried to blend in with the pace of the conversation. But it wasn't easy. I kept wondering if they could tell.

I tried listening to myself, but everything felt a little fuzzy. Was I slurring my words? Getting a bit too animated with my stories? The more I tried to figure it out, the harder it became to be sure.

I took another sip of wine. Okay, this feels fine. Maybe I'm still alright. But the more I thought about it, the more I realised: when it comes to figuring out your level of drunk, you're never quite sure until you've passed the point of no return.

I guess you've been there too. It's easy to feel lost without feedback, especially when it comes to knowing how much is too much. Perhaps you've wondered why some people can control their drinking effortlessly, while others struggle? To understand this and find a path to make lasting change, let's move away from the complex human body and seek insight from a much simpler model. Let's look at how we regulate a vehicle's speed.

Measure the Quantity

To control something, you need to be able to measure it. To control your speed in a car, you start by looking at the speedometer.

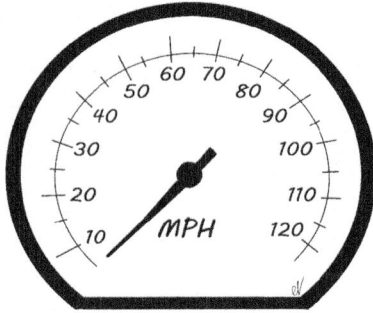

It tells you how fast you're going and how much you're over or under your desired speed. But it doesn't do anything about it. It won't help you avoid a speeding ticket.

Determine the Goal

You have to decide what you want to achieve. Suppose you want to keep your speed at 70mph. A primitive system would monitor your speed, detect if you're travelling below or above 70mph, and alert you when that happens.

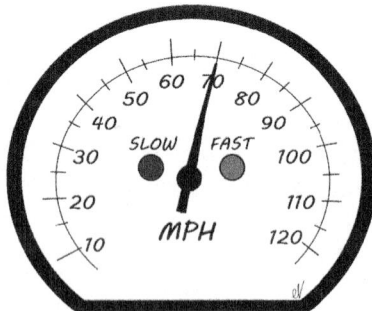

Whenever the FAST light comes on, you apply the brake to slow down. Whenever the SLOW light comes on, you press the throttle to speed up.

Negative Feedback

A cruise control system automates this process by automatically maintaining a set speed, using the speedometer for input. The official term for this is 'negative feedback'. The feedback is 'negative' because the required action is the *opposite* of the condition that triggered it. If the car goes too fast, it slows us down. If the car is too slow, it speeds us up.

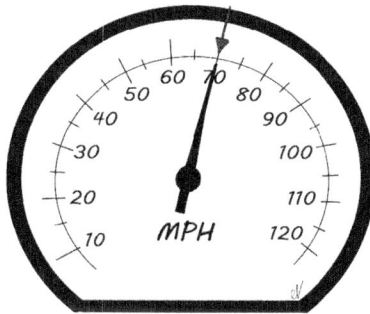

Most well-managed systems have negative feedback built in. The quarterly budget reviews in my corporate job were one such system. Whenever we started to spend more money than planned on a project, we looked for areas where we could make savings. At other times when we used less than forecast, we sought new places to spend the extra money (use it or lose it!).

Look around and you'll find negative feedback in every corner of your life. But how often do you hear people talking about it? It sounds like something has gone wrong if you give negative feedback.

Avoid Positive Feedback

Now let's look at the other side of the coin: positive feedback, which, despite its name, can provoke catastrophes when employed in a control system. Positive feedback basically says: 'Whatever you're doing, keep doing it.' So a cross-wired cruise control system would go faster when you reached your desired speed, or slower when you were below it. In my corporate job, if I discovered I was overspending on a project and decided to spend more, I could drive the business to insolvency.

Despite the confusing names, once you see the effect of positive and negative feedback in the world, you'll never be able to un-see it.

All-or-Nothing Versus Proportional Control

Whether the cruise control is wired correctly for negative feedback or incorrectly for positive feedback, it's a blunt form of control. Nothing happens until the speed wanders, and then it kicks in. It's an all-or-nothing approach to control.

Proportional control is when action is taken in proportion to any deviation. We do this naturally when we drive. If you find you're drifting a little to the right, you steer a little to the left and vice versa. An all-or-nothing driving style would be to allow the car to veer to the opposite side of the road before abruptly yanking the steering wheel to return to your lane. In the corporate world it's the difference between slashing costs in a sales slowdown (possibly further damaging sales), compared to proportionately reducing expenses to reflect lower income.

Proportional control makes systems run more smoothly than all or nothing. I think it is no coincidence that many biological systems are proportional. If the weather turns cold, you'll put on a pullover. If you get very cold, you'll start to shiver - your body's way of generating kinetic energy to warm you up.

Despite most organic systems employing proportional control, many social systems are all or nothing, ping-ponging between extremes. Politics, fashion, diets, drinking! Skinny jeans to flares. Republican to Democrat. You want to drink less but think it's impossible, so you go on a binge. Understanding these control systems can help us develop more effective strategies for managing our drinking and our relationship with ourselves.

Three Possible Outcomes

One of the things I picked up from working around engineers in tech companies for years is that all systems do one of three things: crash, oscillate or stay about the same. Once you understand feedback this becomes clear. If a system crashes, positive feedback is at play. A system that stays about the same is governed by negative feedback. If it oscillates, either negative or positive feedback can be in charge. Feedback doesn't cover everything, but it illustrates a lot.

What does this have to do with you being able to go into a

bar and have just one drink? The problem isn't *drinking less*, it's *drinking too much.* Anyone can drink less... for a while. Many of us have cut back at various times, only to resume drinking too much soon after. So we want to focus on getting our drinking under *control.* Let's take a look at how these three types of behaviour - stability, oscillation and runaway escalation - show up in human behaviour.

Take-It-Or-Leave-It Theresa

We all know someone like Take-It-Or-Leave-It Theresa: the annoying friend who never gets drunk, who drinks socially at parties without overdoing it, who can't understand how anyone could struggle with control. How does she do it?

Theresa is blessed with a built-in Off Switch: a proportional negative feedback loop between her body and her desire to drink. At a party, Theresa takes a glass of champagne to join in. As the evening progresses, her desire signals when it's time to call it a night, even as you plough your way through two bottles. It's effortless for her. Desire is the key factor. Theresa's feedback system connects drinks consumed to her level of inner desire, *not to external factors* like joining in or missing out.

Seesawing Sean

Maybe you can relate to Sean, or at least know someone like him. Sean is always trying to cut back - effectively on a permanent drinking diet - counting days sober until a bad day at work leads him to "drown his sorrows." Sean is struggling with a different feedback system.

Unlike Theresa's proportional negative feedback system, Sean's is all or nothing, swinging from a series of alcohol free days until he thinks he deserves a reward and finds himself with a hangover. Having lived like this for many years, Sean believes there's only one solution: sobriety, because moderation is clearly not something he's capable of. So, for the millionth time, he gets back on the wagon, announces "Day 1," fingers crossed behind his back - never believing it will come to anything.

Cutting back is miserable for Sean. In order to drink less, he has to fight his cravings for beer and hope that he can muster enough willpower to get through another day. Over the years, Sean has incorporated this struggle into his identity: "If I try to moderate it doesn't last. One drink leads to another and another until I've downed a couple of bottles. The torture of wondering if I have embarrassed myself begins all over again. There's nothing for it but to endure sobriety because moderating is just impossible for someone like me."

What Sean doesn't realise is that his problem is simply poor (positive) feedback. If he got accurate (negative) feedback, like Theresa, he'd never drink too much or need willpower to stay sober.

Overdrinking Olive

Olive would pay to be Sean. Olive consistently overdrinks and with each passing year is drinking more. First it was a few glasses, then a bottle, and now she'd rather not think about it. She's mostly healthy, but worries about the long-term effects of her drinking and envies those who drink less. If only there were a way. She's been on the hamster wheel of commitment, weakening resolve, and failure to control her drinking for years. Why is it so hard for her?

The answer is it's all down to her feedback system. Olive doesn't register when she's had too much. She's used to pouring a drink, checking out, and only coming back to reality when the glass is empty and it's time to decide whether to have another. Nothing tells her to stop. Unlike Sean who occasionally overdrinks, Olive is like a runaway train, unable to control herself.

If you relate to Olive, you might wonder, "What's wrong with me?" Hear me when I say: "Nothing." You have no character flaw. Your feedback system is simply wired up wrong. You have a positive feedback loop that says "if you have one drink keep on drinking."

Change Your Feedback System

Olive's drinking problem, like Seesawing Sean's, stems from relying on faulty feedback. To solve the problem she doesn't need to feel guilty or judge herself, she simply needs a functioning Off Switch to provide the proportional negative feedback she lacks.

If you're still unconvinced, consider life before hearing aids. Poor hearing was unchangeable, so people might have been told to practice listening! Today, if Olive were born with poor hearing, she'd wear a hearing aid and neither you nor she would think anything of it. She'd laugh at any suggestion she ditch her hearing aid and just try to get more willpower to improve her hearing.

Building an Off Switch to counteract faulty feedback is an effective way to give Olive back control over her drinking.

Recap

We've covered a lot of ground, so let's pause for a quick recap. We've explored the benefits of an Off Switch - to drink in a way that you choose, even if you don't yet know how to build one.

In chapter two, we learned why and how we get into the unintentional habit of drinking too much. Further, we discovered that to get control of our drinking we need to first get authority over our desire, which stems from our thoughts.

In this chapter, we learned how negative feedback explains why some people struggle with drinking too much while others can take it or leave it. An effective Off Switch will provide feedback to stabilise the system, helping you achieve and maintain your desired relationship with alcohol.

All the information in the world, however, won't change a thing unless you're willing to take action based upon it. It's time to build your Off Switch.

CHAPTER FOUR

Step 1: Plan

I clearly remember the quarterly operations meeting when the engineering division presented its launch plan for a new entry-level design product to Exec Staff. This was a high stakes presentation. This team's products had historically been responsible for 70% of corporate revenue, but the last three quarters hadn't been strong.

The presentation started well. The new product projections were impressive - the numbers seemed to promise nothing short of success, with loads of market research backing them up. The marketing strategy seemed as water-tight as the best marketing strategy could be. And the production timeline? Detailed and clear. Every 'i' was dotted, every 't' crossed. The slides were polished, the divisional VP exuded confidence, and the room hummed with approval.

The head of international sales leaned back with a Cheshire-cat grin and said, "If everything goes right, this could be huge."

His words hung in the air, but then my boss raised his hand and asked, "And what's our strategy if things don't go to plan?"

I wasn't surprised. In our division we had a plan for everything: vendor contracts, launches, customer complaints, vacation scheduling. My boss lived and breathed the famous mantra: 'By failing to plan, you are planning to fail.'

So it is fitting that the first component of your Off Switch is writing a drink plan - the cornerstone to achieving control. Yes, I'm going to teach you how to plan.

But I don't teach planning like most people. You are NOT going to plan some rubbish that's hard to follow. You're not going to set some arbitrary drinks limit that you think sounds good or which you figure you *should* be able to stick to. You're not going to *hope* (cross fingers) you could stick to your plan. You're not going to use willpower to fight your way to your goal.

The Off Switch: How It Works

PLAN DRINKS
(How much? Why?)

EVALUATE & LEARN
(What worked? What didn't?)

EMBRACE CRAVINGS
(Stop, Look, Listen)

Instead you are going to set a 24 hour *realistic* plan. A plan you are *willing* to follow - no matter who you're with, no matter what you're doing, no matter how you're feeling, no matter how many (or few) drinks you plan. No matter any of it. You will simply be willing to follow through on what you have decided in advance.

In fact, *the number of drinks on your plan is far less important than the way you think about, approach and execute your plan.* This is especially true at the start because a drink plan is about building trust with yourself. This makes a huge difference for so many people so I want you to have it.

Why Plan Drinks?

Planning drinks may seem weird, unnecessary or restrictive, especially at first. You may feel it stamps out the spontaneity that makes life fun. I think you'll find the reality isn't that bad, but you may be asking why anyone would want to do that and how it could possibly help. So let's start there. We'll explore why planning your drinks makes all the difference and how to do it effectively.

The main goal of a drink plan is to bring intention and awareness to what is often an unconscious habit. By planning drinks, you eliminate the need for on-the-fly decisions about what, when and how much to drink. If you take nothing else away from this book, write a drink plan.

We plan all sorts of stuff every day - holidays, car maintenance, grocery shopping - to ensure we get our desired result ... Yet by "winging it" when it comes to alcohol, making every decision on the spur of the moment, you're placing your health in the hands of a process that you *know* inevitably leads to serious trouble. A process that you have no faith or trust in. So why do we do this? The top three reasons I hear time and again are:

1. We want to be spontaneous and have a drink if we feel like it.
2. We worry that a drink plan complicates our lives by having to decide ahead of time how much will be 'enough.'
3. We fear that writing a drink plan is proof that we "have a problem" and must, therefore, be "an alcoholic."

In chapter two we saw that to change your relationship with alcohol you need to think about it differently. So let's start by considering three alternatives to the above:

1. Being spontaneous - ie letting yourself have a drink if you feel like it - is what has led to the overdrinking. A drink plan, on the other hand, creates structure around alcohol leaving spontaneity to other *more important* areas of your life: to read a book after dinner; to jump in a car and visit a friend on a whim; to work on an art project when inspiration strikes.

2.   A drink plan *simplifies* your life and saves time because it eliminates the nightly "Should I drink?" "Maybe I could have just one?" "Or maybe I shouldn't?" negotiations.

3.   You don't fear you're a a bad cook if you follow a recipe; you don't consider yourself an unskilled driver when you plan your routes; you're not a poor public speaker if you write your speeches in advance. So a drink plan is no different than any other plan: it sets expectations and saves you time in the moment.

How to Write a Drink Plan

So how do you start? Writing a daily drink plan is a simple process that, with practice, will only take about three minutes. Three minutes! Taken in the context of the 1,440 minutes you have available each day, this time investment is a small price to pay for feeling in control of your life. To write a drink plan, you answer four questions:

1.   When is the plan for?
2.   What will you drink?
3.   How much will you drink?
4.   Why are you choosing to drink?

1. When Is the Plan For?

Each drink plan covers a 24-hour period. To get started, I recommend planning your drinks one day at a time. This gives you a clearer picture of your day and helps you focus on what feels realistic, without getting lost by looking too far ahead. This increases the likelihood that you'll stick to your plan and reduces any resistance to planning drinks by eliminating the excuse that you "don't have a crystal ball and can't predict the future!"

As you get more comfortable and experienced with drink planning, you may find it preferable to plan a week at a time. But to start, always write daily plans.

24 Hours In Advance

You will use your prefrontal cortex (see chapter two) for this task as it excels at intentional planning and making decisions for the long-term. Since your prefrontal cortex operates more slowly than your pleasure-loving lizard brain, write your drink plans 24 hours in advance. So you'll write Wednesday's plan on Tuesday, Thursday's plan on Wednesday, and so on.

A Regular Schedule

I recommend setting a regular schedule to write your drink plan - it's a great way to build the habit. Try pairing it with a daily pattern you already have, like after breakfast or brushing your teeth. Writing your drink plan is a powerful, positive habit that will completely transform your drinking. Start as you mean to go on and set yourself up for success.

A Positive Addition

Your attitude toward drink planning will have a big impact on your results. The more you see planning as a positive addition to your life, not something to endure, the more successful you'll be. By consciously and consistently deciding when, what, and why you will drink, rather than drinking by default, you're building a more intentional and clear relationship with alcohol.

Many of my clients go further and use drink plans alongside other life decisions like setting a sleep schedule or planning weekly meals. Time and again, these are the ones who transform their relationship with alcohol the fastest.

2. What Will You Drink?

You might be wondering what's the best way to write a drink plan, what drinks you should include and how many.

There are no right answers to these questions, but remember that your goal is to write a plan you are *willing* to follow. The drinks you put on your plan are 100% up to you. You likely already have your go-to brew so start with that. Whatever your usual choice of drink, I do recommend you pay attention to the alcohol by volume (ABV), as it indicates the drink's strength. The hard stuff is called that for a reason: you get drunk faster on spirits than beer and wine. The Off Switch app separates beer, wine and spirits because of the difference in ABV.

No Precise Order Needed

Deciding the precise order of drinks isn't crucial. For example, you might plan a gin and tonic as an aperitif, followed by two glasses of wine with dinner. But it's fine to have the gin and tonic after dinner instead. You want to develop a plan that provides guidance while allowing some flexibility in execution. So worry less about the order of drinks than what you actually drink and your willingness to follow through.

3. How Much Will You Drink?

When deciding how many drinks to include in your plan, it can be tempting to rely solely on external guidelines - like government recommendations - or to create strict personal rules, such as 'no drinking on weekdays' or 'no drinks before 8pm unless it's a special occasion.' While these can be helpful starting points, avoid aiming for a 'perfect' plan, because this can backfire. *Trying* to stick to unrealistic rules often leads to frustration and annoyance, you wonder why you thought this was a good idea, you convince yourself you'll never change and it's never going to work ... so you give up on planning altogether. We aren't going to do that.

Keep things simple, especially at first. Focus on writing plans that feel achievable and sustainable - even if the little voice in your head keeps insisting you *should* be able to do better. Let that voice jabber on while you focus on writing plans you can *trust* yourself to follow, not those which require willpower to maintain. Rather than immediately forcing yourself to plan alcohol free nights, for example, focus on what you're realistically *willing* to commit to. This way you'll be planning for the real world, not the perfect world.

I recommend you start by planning the exact same amount you would normally drink, then begin to reduce the quantity when you feel ready. If this feels too easy, that's the point. It's meant to. Besides it feels *totally different* to drink to a plan than to wing it. You'll experience so much more control, even if the actual amount is the same as usual. Wild but true.

Do this on repeat and you will build up your sense of self-trust. You will start to see yourself as someone who follows through on their plans. Your self-confidence will grow. This has a huge impact on your ability to drink differently. By starting with doable goals, you'll build the belief, resilience and habits necessary to achieve long-term success. You won't fight yourself nor worry about feeling deprived. You'll start to see what you're capable of. You'll plan fewer drinks naturally and willingly. You'll be in a new cycle of feeling in control.

Consistent Serving Sizes

Stick to consistent serving sizes, measuring by the glass in whole numbers (one bottle of beer equals one glass). The exact volume (175ml, 250ml, 8oz, ...) doesn't matter as long as you're consistent. When dining out, refuse top-ups and stick to whole glasses to maintain control. You can always request a refill when you're ready for your next planned drink.

Alcohol Free (AF) Days

I recommend you also write drink plans for alcohol free (AF) days. Instead of contemplating how empty life will be without drinking, ask what you're going to fill it with instead? Documenting your reasons for not drinking can serve as a powerful motivator and reinforce your commitment to why you are choosing to not drink.

Beware of Manipulating Your Plans

Remember, it is not a rule or law to write a drink plan; it is your choice. View it as an opportunity to make decisions for yourself, not as a restriction. The goal is to decide what you'll drink then stick to it. Don't try to 'game' the system by planning smaller servings and overfilling the glasses; instead, plan for the actual amount you intend to drink. If you think this is a way to get more wine by choosing ultra large glasses, you're missing the point. The size of the serving doesn't matter - what's important is making conscious decisions in advance using your prefrontal cortex. This will avoid you sneaking around your plans and drinking behind your own back. We're aiming for openness, consistency and clarity.

Managing Expectations

After the initial excitement ("I'm finally doing something about my drinking!") wears off, you might feel impatient for faster progress. You might be tempted to plan more alcohol free days than you've had in a decade. Or some equally ambitious target. Don't. It ends where you've already been: abandoned commitments, broken promises and plummeting self-confidence. Instead, continue to make doable drink plans, focusing on what you're *willing* to aim for. Be prepared to feel underwhelmed at times, but concentrate on growing your confidence. Remember, the goal is not a temporary fix, but a lasting change in your relationship with alcohol.

You Don't Have to Drink It All

Sometimes you'll plan drinks and just not feel like having them. Or you'll plan three glasses and feel happy to stop after one. That's okay. You do not have to drink every drink on the plan! Just make sure you truly don't want the drinks, rather than simply convincing yourself that you *shouldn't* have them. The intention behind these thoughts makes a big difference.

Whenever this happens it's a great opportunity to ask why you think you have no desire in that moment. Is there something you can learn from this? Have you done something differently? Even little changes count. It's important to not write these days off as flukes that "just happened." As we saw in chapter 2, things never just happen. Every action is preceded by a thought and a feeling. So get curious and find out why everything went well today. This information will come in handy when things aren't feeling so easy.

4. Why Are You Choosing to Drink?

This is the most important question on the drink plan. *Do not skip this step.* You may find this question difficult to answer, especially at first. You might be tempted to say, "I don't know why I want to drink. I just do." But stick with it. Understanding why you want to drink reinforces that you are treating it as a conscious decision instead of as an automatic habit.

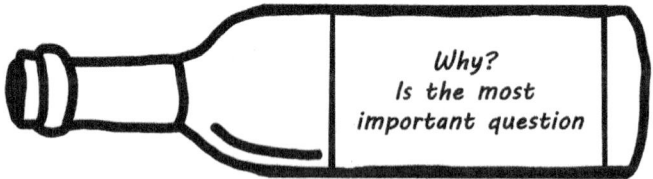

Why? Is the most important question

Your reason why doesn't have to be earth-shattering, but it has to resonate with you. Avoid writing the same thing every day or it will feel meaningless. Use this as an opportunity to get to know yourself. If you're stuck for ideas, consider things like: "Because this is part of the process," "Because I'm interested to see how differently I feel when I plan," or "Because I'm experimenting."

As you become more adept at writing drink plans, I

encourage you to ask yourself if you *like* your reasons. For instance, you might write that you want to drink, "Because it's Friday and I always drink on Fridays," but is that a reason you *like*? Do you want to be the kind of person who drinks because it's Friday? Maybe yes, maybe no. There are no good or bad, right or wrong reasons. There are just the ones you like and the ones you don't. It's really worth spending time on this, because I have found that the amount of positive enjoyment you get from your choices and the strength of the self-trust you build is linked to how you feel about your 'why.'

While we're on this topic, if your drink plan 'why' is, "Because I want to escape my life," I will offer this: you don't need more ways to escape, you need a different life. Drinking less isn't just about cutting back - it's the key to unlocking a whole new way of living.

View from the Trend

In the early days of drink planning your results may seem contradictory and confusing. You may not feel as though you're making enough progress. You may be so deep in the details of drink planning that you don't see the longer-term identity shifts that are happening. It's time to look at the trend line.

A trend line shows the overall direction in which a situation is developing. Consider the stock market. The price of a stock may vary enormously over a day, but investors don't want all the details; they just need to know the trending health of their investment. They get this from a trend line because it can do only one of three things: Go up, go down, or stay the same.

What's good for the stock market is good for us. The trend line feature in the Off Switch app (see Appendix) is a valuable tool for monitoring your progress. Do not underestimate the value of a trend line. It smooths out daily fluctuations, making it easier to see the direction of travel. It's a powerful psychological tool that not only gives you a more accurate picture of your progress over time, but it will motivate you to keep going. It also serves as an early warning system if the trend starts to go up.

While you're writing plans to drink less, you'll observe a downward trend in the chart. If you start to 'cheat' a bit here or there, the upward direction of the trend line will make it easy to see what's happening and diagnose the cause, even if the day-to-day changes are subtle. Once you've stabilised the ship and reached your desired relationship with alcohol, the trend line will appear constant (neither up nor down).

There is also a trend line that shows your planning accuracy - are you regularly hitting your drink plans or not? This is such an important measure. The more you trust yourself to hit your drink plans the more you'll trust yourself to actually follow through on what you planned.

By following the trend line, you'll have a clear understanding of your progress and won't overlook minor changes that could impact your goals.

Perhaps You're Wondering …

Here are the most frequently asked questions or concerns I hear about drink planning.

"Will I Always Have to Write Drink Plans?"

I always answer this with another question: why *wouldn't* you want to? Writing plans makes drinking intentional and mindful. They will help you achieve your desired relationship with alcohol. And they will help you to maintain it by providing structure and preventing occasional 'one-off' drinks from escalating over time.

Let's consider what happens when you stop writing drink plans… You stop being intentional. When you stop being intentional, you give free rein to your lizard brain's impulsive tendencies. Even small changes, such as two to three extra drinks per week, can disrupt your rhythm. The changes will be subtle. You may be unaware of them at first, but when you do notice you will feel awful: not just hungover, but persecuted and powerless. And all from an extra glass or two here or there that grew over time.

If you had continued to plan your drinks this would never have happened. Any increase in consumption would be evident in your plans and reflected in your trend line. A drink plan doesn't have to be intrusive or interfere with your enjoyment; instead view it as a safety net. So really, why wouldn't you continue with drink plans? If you want to keep alcohol in your life, even moderately, I recommend you always write a drink plan.

"I Don't Know What I'm Doing Tomorrow."

This thought is very common and is just your brain making an excuse. Whether you'll be at home, out with others, at the beach, or at a company event doesn't matter. You're learning to drink with intention, not reacting to the moment. Whatever you plan will be 'enough' if that's what you decide. So write your drink plan as usual, making a best guess if you feel uncertain, and commit to following it regardless of your circumstances.

"I Don't Know What the Others Want to Do."

Don't make other people's plans central to your decision. Write your drink plan as usual and decide you'll make it work. You don't control other people. They may tell you one thing and they may change their minds. Remember, they have lizard brains too! Instead, decide what you want for yourself, no matter what other people may do.

"I Think Drink Plans Are Stupid and Unnecessary."

If you're reluctant to write a drink plan or find them pointless, ask yourself: would you rather drink intentionally or worry about overdoing things like before? Look for the upsides. Focus on how they're helpful. Loving your plan increases the likelihood you'll stick to it and achieve long-term success. Resistance to planning is your lizard brain acting the toddler, demanding chocolate for dinner instead of carrots.

"Can I Change My Drink Plan at the Last Minute?"

Picture this: You've written your plan, you're solid on it, but as the evening approaches, you start to reconsider your options. Despite there being no good reason to change your plan, you feel tempted to do so. This is very common and one of the top reasons why people struggle with control.

If this happens to you, remind yourself that this mental negotiation is just your lizard brain at work. You had the opportunity to decide a rational plan. You chose this one with your prefrontal cortex - the part of your brain that wants the best for you. Don't alter it now, no matter how much your pleasure-seeking, consequence-averse lizard brain tries to influence you. (Besides, you can always plan to drink the alcohol tomorrow. Just not today.)

CHAPTER FIVE

Step 2: Embrace

Annual product launch events were a standing feature of the corporate calendar. As the head of a division, my attendance at them was required. Despite how much I dreaded the social grind, I soon became a seasoned pro at mingling with thousands of reseller partners and customers, packed with handshakes, schmoozing, and

endless small talk. Over time, I developed a routine: grab a glass (or two) of white wine to take the edge off, and get through the night. It wasn't glamorous, but it worked.

Until the year my plan fell apart. I arrived, headed for the bar and discovered the only white wine on offer was undrinkable. (Think vinegar and you're on the right track.) The red wasn't an option for me either, so for the first time I had to wing it without my usual crutch. I settled on sparkling water, convinced it was going to be the longest, most uncomfortable night ever.

But here's the thing - it wasn't. Without the wine, I stayed sharper, more present, and oddly enough, more at ease. I ended up having some genuinely engaging conversations, the kind where you're actually paying attention to what the other person's saying, rather than distractedly 'suffering' them and looking over their shoulder for an escape route. I'd known a lot of these people for years, but this was the first time I felt like I had real conversations with any of them...

Was it fun? No, I wouldn't go that far. But it also wasn't the social disaster I'd braced myself for. In fact, in some ways, it was better. That night taught me something surprising: maybe wine wasn't the 'must-have' I'd always believed it to be. That I wasn't as socially anxious as I'd always claimed. That when I accepted a situation for what it was, I no longer even craved wine. This made me wonder - where else in my life might wine no longer be as necessary as I thought? What else could I try?

So what else could *you* try? Let's turn our attention to cravings - that urgent desire for wine that shows up each day at 6pm on the dot or which seems to come from nowhere when your friend drops by and casually asks, "Fancy a drink?"

Common wisdom encourages a 'fight or flight' reaction when temptation strikes - to grit your teeth through the craving (resist), keep your hands busy during the so-called 'witching hour' (distract) or hide away to prevent yourself feeling triggered in the first place (avoid). Perhaps these have been your go-to responses until now? How are they working out for you? Exactly. So we're going to take an altogether different approach.

We'll go *towards* cravings. We're going to feel them and *fully embrace* them. "Whaaat?" You might be thinking, "That sounds like a terrible idea." I realise it's unconventional, but stick with me because this one thing will blow your mind and change your life. When you stop making cravings the bad guy, you reduce your desire, silence the mental chatter and make it easier to stick to your drink plans. Welcome to the second component of your Off Switch - tackling cravings with the Stop, Look and Listen process.

The Off Switch: How It Works

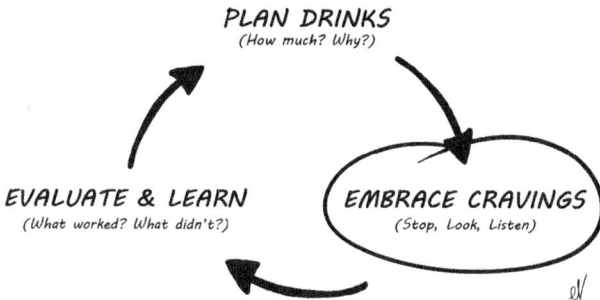

PLAN DRINKS
(How much? Why?)

EVALUATE & LEARN
(What worked? What didn't?)

EMBRACE CRAVINGS
(Stop, Look, Listen)

As we saw in chapter two, cravings are simply *feelings of desire designed to motivate you to take action*. Whether you consider a craving to be a problem or not depends on your perspective. If you're struggling with your weight, you might dread the pull of chocolate biscuits. But if you're effortlessly slim, you would think nothing of indulging in a sweet snack. Take-it-or-leave-it Theresa won't think twice about ordering a glass of rosé, while you might tear your hair out over your lack of control.

Cravings Hold No Authority

The most important thing I want you to know is that you needn't fear cravings, because they *hold no authority over you unless you decide to act*. While you may feel uncomfortable during a craving - perhaps experiencing shortness of breath, tingling cheeks, or a dry mouth - there's nothing to fear because these are all just *feelings*. A craving itself is harmless; the challenge lies in managing your *response* to it.

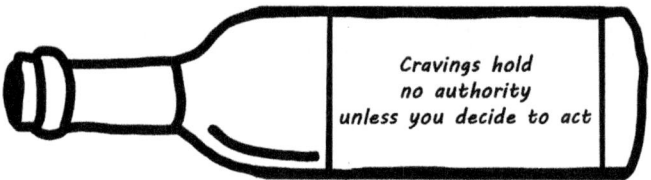

Cravings hold
no authority
unless you decide to act

Think of a craving as a toddler throwing a tantrum for a chocolate bar in a crowded shop. You know you don't have to give in to their demands; you just need to wait for the outburst to burn itself out. The difficulty lies in how you *feel* in that moment. All eyes on you. The tut-tutting judgment from strangers. The discomfort. The embarrassment.

And so it is with a craving. Not complying with a craving is straightforward - you simply don't drink the wine or eat the cookie. The real challenge is dealing with the emotions that arise from *not* drinking the wine and *not* eating the cookie: the sense of deprivation, of feeling denied, restricted and excluded. It's no surprise that sooner or later we give in, then rationalise our behaviour by saying things like, "That's just how I am" or "I always pour a glass when I'm stressed." We act as if the craving is irresistible, as if it's something we must obey - but the more we give in, the more *we prove to ourselves* that we have no power. We become better at doing the thing we don't want to do and reinforce our (unwanted) default behaviour. Happily it is within your easy control to change this.

From this moment on I want you to remember that cravings do not signify some innate need. You were not born with a desire for wine. It is simply a learned response that became habitual over time. This chapter will show you how to take control of your choices and overcome your cravings by following the Stop, Look, Listen process.

How NOT to Handle Cravings

First let's explore why the usual fight or flight approaches to cravings (resist, avoid and distract) don't work over the long-term.

Resist

Resistance is the most commonly recommended approach. You know you're resisting cravings when you use tough, battle language to fight the desire. You might say things like, "The cravings are coming, I've just gotta be strong" or "If I can just resist until 6pm, I'll be fine." You may give yourself a pep talk or repeat a mantra like, "I will not drink tonight whatever it takes!" but no matter what you tell yourself (and even if you succeed for a while), you will eventually get worn down and give in ... because it's exhausting to battle cravings. Every time you resist a craving you fight yourself - and inadvertently make the thing you're resisting *irresistible*.

This is why you can resist a cookie for days on end, only to demolish an entire packet in one sitting, or why you'll go three weeks without wine, then have a bad day and drink two bottles.

Distract

Distraction is another widely recommended technique. How often have you heard, "Just distract yourself from the wine witch!" Aside from the fact that there is no such thing as the wine witch (!), distraction is about filling up your time so you don't feel the feelings that come up. Popular distraction techniques include going to the gym, knitting, doing crosswords or taking the dog for a walk. This strategy may work in the short term, but is flawed as a permanent solution (unless you want to forever fill your time in this way). Remaining on guard against such temptations is exhausting - and what happens if you're at a wedding or a company 'do' where you couldn't whip out your knitting? You won't have the skills to handle the situation. Sooner or later you'll give in and drink.

Important side note: there's nothing wrong with going to the gym, taking the dog for a walk and all the other things as long as you're not doing them *expressly* to distract yourself from drinking.

Avoid

When you avoid cravings, it's like you're trying to control your environment in order to be successful. You might go to bed early, decline party invitations, remove alcohol from the house, or demand that your husband stops drinking around you. This can work for a while, but it's not a sustainable approach to lasting change, because you can't avoid the outside world forever. Sooner or later, you'll be faced with a situation where you'll feel triggered. Your wife arrives home with a surprise bottle of wine. A hotel offers complimentary champagne at dinner. You're on an upgraded flight with free-flowing cocktails. If you spend your time avoiding cravings, you won't develop the skills to handle these situations, so you'll likely crack, give in and drink.

What Eventually Happens …

So there you have it. If you resist, avoid or distract yourself from cravings, it is highly likely that sooner or later you will find yourself drinking again. Often more than before. I say this on good authority: it is the most common experience of my clients when they first come to me. There are two main reasons for this:

First, it's hard to always be resisting or distracting yourself or avoiding situations where there may be alcohol. Your life will feel like one long battle. It's exhausting, overwhelming and not at all fun! We humans are not designed to be in a permanent state of fight/flight/freeze. We can only take those negative feelings for so long before we do the one thing we've taught ourselves provides relief: drink.

Second, every time you do eventually give in and drink, you are rewarding the craving. In that moment you're telling your brain, "Yes, this works, this feels good. Let's do this again anytime we feel exhausted or overwhelmed or frustrated ....” So the next time you're feeling negative emotions your brain sends cravings your way to motivate you to pour the wine. This is when people tell me, "I tried my best to resist but deep down I knew I was going to drink." And so the cycle continues.

What to Do Instead

Resistance, distraction and avoidance may offer temporary success for handling cravings, but do not work over the long-term. So what *does*?

Going *towards* the craving, not running from it. Allowing it to just be there. Being willing to fully *embrace* it. (Yes, really!) When you do this you stop making the craving a problem. By no longer battling it, running from it or pretending it's not there, you get authority over it, over yourself and what you do when you feel this way.

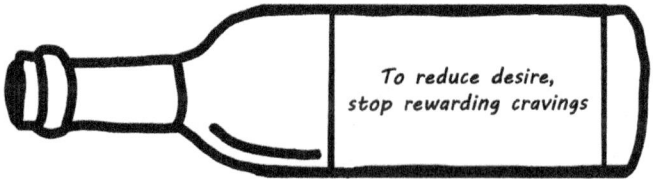

To reduce desire, stop rewarding cravings

What does this mean in practice? It's about allowing yourself to really, really *want* the alcohol, to *feel* the desire coursing through you - but to not drink. Imagine I put a glass of your favourite wine or beer right in front of you. Instead of yelling, "Get that away from me!" you let yourself want, want, want the drink - but you don't pick it up and you don't drink it.

This is how you embrace a craving and how you stop rewarding the desire you feel with the thing it's seeking (the alcohol). Practice this again and again and you will reduce your desire, the cravings will stop and it will feel easy to be around alcohol.

This will take effort, practice and time. Expect it to feel uncomfortable. Plan on the cravings appearing in the usual places at the usual times. *Expect* your brain to say, "It's time to drink! Where's the wine? I need to get the wine!" When this happens, fully embrace the craving and wait until it leaves of its own accord. It will, I promise. Just as a toddler's temper tantrum always burns itself out eventually.

You may have many cravings, one after the other. This may feel exhausting at first, but as with anything, it gets easier the more you practice. The intensity and quantity of your cravings will start to decrease *when your brain learns that you don't reward the craving and drink every time you feel desire.* Repeatedly embracing cravings ultimately translates into no cravings.

Stop, Look, Listen

But how do you let yourself feel the desire without actually drinking? If you're thinking this sounds easier said than done, I've got you. Just follow this 3-step 'Stop, Look, Listen' process.

Stop

The first step is to gain awareness. To become adept at noticing *when* you're having a craving, including all the subtle little ones that can slip under the radar. This could be anything from, "I want a drink now!" to a growing sense of anticipation as you drive home from work, or the mental gymnastics of going back and forth on whether or not you should open a bottle tonight.

I want you to notice when this happens and *pause.*

Counting to ten can help. Then infuse each of these moments with *awareness*. This could be as simple as saying aloud, "I'm having a craving," "This is what a craving feels like," or "Cravings are normal … nothing has gone wrong."

This may sound silly. You may feel silly doing it. You may be tempted to skip this step. Don't. Consciously recognising your cravings is powerful because *every time you pause, you interrupt the habit*. Every. Single. Time. Just this one thing will take the drinking off autopilot - the first step to regaining control.

Look

When you create the pause, you have the opportunity to explore your motivations. While your surface level thought might be, "A drink would be nice," deeper factors are at play. Your beliefs about why you drink too much, why you think alcohol helps, the emotions you want to escape and how you want to feel - these are all contained within a craving.

Most of us overlook this wealth of information because we're so used to focusing on the negative consequences of drinking too much or trying to grit our teeth to get through the craving. Instead, get curious and ask yourself what's really going on.

Remember there are two parts to a craving: thoughts in your head and sensations in your body. The mental back-and-forth of "Should I drink or not?" is often the most distressing part so get out of this drama by dropping into your body and becoming an observer of yourself. Imagine you're a scientist studying your own behaviour, neutrally and with curiosity.

Alternatively, visualise yourself as a toy where you can pop your head off and set it to one side while you focus on your body from the neck down. This directs you from the drama and you'll see what's factually happening. This is a powerful way to interrupt the automatic habit cycle.

What's happening in my body?

See yourself breathing through the feeling and ask, "What am I feeling right now?" Then drop into your body and notice where you physically feel the craving. Is there tension in the shoulders? A sensation in the pit of your stomach? Do you feel restless? Are your hands tingling? Is your face flushed? Be as objective as possible in these observations.

Our brains love to answer questions. Left to their own devices they'll keep asking the same ones ("Why am I such a screw up?... Why can't I ever learn?") so do yourself a favour and set them to work on topics that will move you in a new direction. Questions like: What do I think the drink will provide? Why do I feel I need a reward right now? Why does this drink feel necessary?

Getting curious will teach you so much about your motivations and patterns. When my clients answer these questions for the first time, they often shock themselves at the words which come out of their mouths. It's as though they're learning (and hearing!) their true intentions for the first time. Which they often are.

Listen

Next, listen to yourself. This is where you uncover the true nature of your desire. While you may think you're drooling at the idea of your favourite cocktail, your brain is seeing more than just a drink. It's telling you things like:

- You're tired and want to put your feet up.
- A drink will help you tolerate your family!
- Come on, you deserve to stop feeling so responsible for a couple of hours.

Learning to listen to what's really happening in your mind is a skill that requires practice. You are likely not used to pausing and questioning your feelings, let alone listening to the answers. While you can't force yourself to not want something that you want, if you stay patient and conscious, this becomes a gentle process of letting go.

The more you practice, the more skilled you'll become. You'll learn what you're really seeking when you pour a drink. You'll stop judging your feelings. You'll start considering other ways to give yourself what you're seeking. You'll start to feel more in charge and more in control. This alone will change your life.

Learning to listen to yourself is a skill

Curiosity Rules the Roost

The aim of Stop, Look, Listen is to have a conversation with yourself. It's a way to cultivate curiosity about your habit and to uncover what's lurking beneath the surface. You'll come to understand that your brain has learned what a drink represents. It might be how you clock off at the end of the day, reward yourself for a job well done, relax in social settings, or cope with anxiety. You'll identify the emotions you avoid when you have a drink because alcohol numbs them - the stress, anxiety, boredom, all of it. By embracing the craving, you will start to see this. You'll see that you can feel these negative emotions without making any of this a problem.

The same is true on the positive end of the spectrum - when you're using alcohol to enhance an experience, to make it a little bit better. Consider sitting on the deck watching a sunset - wonderful, right? Now consider sitting on the deck watching a sunset thinking, "This would be better with a glass of champagne." As soon as you decide an experience is lacking, your brain will focus on that and you'll actually miss out on the enjoyment available to you in that moment.

When changing a habit it's so important *to pay attention to what you're paying attention to*. The more you use this 3-step process, the more aware you'll become of what's going on beneath the surface. Of everything you're thinking, what you're making that mean, what you're feeling and what you don't want to feel.

When you get curious, understand your desire, go towards cravings and use your prefrontal cortex to get ahead of your lizard brain, then you will bring the internal drink/don't drink conflict to an end. And life will never feel the same again!

Negative Feedback In Action

Embracing cravings is an excellent example of negative feedback (discussed in chapter three) in action. The more you embrace cravings, the less intense they feel. You'll find yourself drinking less in response to the emotion of *want*. It's a brilliant, natural way to quench the flames of desire.

As your cravings reduce in intensity and duration, you'll find it easier to plan fewer drinks. In fact it feels increasingly normal to do so. You'll be done with the all or nothing narrative ("Once I start, I can't stop!") and start rocking proportional control where you see every sip as a decision.

The more willing you are to embrace cravings, the less desire you will feel over time. The more you practise *not resisting, not avoiding, not distracting yourself and not rewarding* the craving with a drink, the easier this becomes. It may feel tedious at times, but just think that every time you repeat this new pattern you are bedding in a new habit.

Also consider how many opportunities you have to practice. For once there's an upside to being a daily drinker!

Count the Cravings

As you use this process, I recommend you track your progress by counting every fully-embraced craving. A tally mark system with pen and paper would do the job, but why not have fun with it? I love gold star charts, like those used in schools, as a motivating tool. Alternatively, you could drop a bead, button, or even a piece of dried pasta into a jar. Watching your progress build up visually can be stimulating and provide a satisfying sense of accomplishment. Record every single embraced craving, even if you experience several small ones in succession.

You can also do this on evenings out without calling attention to yourself. Simply put a number of coins or buttons in one pocket, then each time you embrace a craving you move a coin or button to another pocket. At the end of the evening, count them up and add them to your total.

Imagine the transformation you will experience when you've embraced 100 cravings without drinking. You will have rewired the strong conditioned behaviour that had you drinking on autopilot and you will have created a new, desired habit. You will no longer fear cravings and you will no longer drink without conscious control.

Important counting note: This is not about being perfect. If you successfully embrace some cravings, but then drink, or find yourself reverting to old habits of resisting, avoiding or distracting yourself, do not empty your craving jar or rip the stars from your chart. Just pick up where you left off and keep going. Every embraced craving counts.

Preventing Cravings

This chapter has been about handling cravings. To wrap things up, I want to share a simple but powerful way to help you experience fewer cravings in the first place.

Rather than finding ways to take the edge off, there are things you can do to prevent the edge in the first place. Do this by paying attention to areas of dissatisfaction in your life. Where are you pushing through negative emotions? Where are you tolerating?

Instead of framing your evening glass of wine as your "time to unwind," consider the deeper reasons behind it. When you see a drink as a way to relax, it sends a signal to your brain that you're off the clock - that it's time to put your feet up and truly unwind. So imagine the message your brain receives when you stop drinking at your usual times. It doesn't interpret it as 'no alcohol'; instead, it wonders, "Does this mean we're not doing rest and relaxation anymore?" No wonder it freaks out and sends a craving. This is the way you've taught yourself to cope with stress and relax.

Instead of giving wine the responsibility for how you unwind, focus on looking after yourself. Create pockets of me-time *during the day*. This doesn't have to mean hours of meditation or luxurious spa treatments (though those count too!). Sipping a hot drink without distraction, practicing deep breathing, or listening to a favourite song are great options. The more you take small moments to rest throughout the day, the less you'll feel a strong urge for release - and wine - when 6pm comes around.

Before you tell me this is impossible, ask what have you got to lose? It doesn't matter how busy you are, or how big your job is. Anyone can take a few seconds here or there to focus on their needs. If you really insist it's impossible, start small. Pause right now and give yourself 30 seconds of deep breathing before you read the next sentence. Then build up from there.

The payoff is huge. It's easy to implement. You'll see a direct effect on the number and intensity of your cravings. Plus it's something you can start immediately.

CHAPTER SIX

Step 3: Evaluate

Have you ever overslept on a day that could make or break your career? If so you're in good company. One unforgettable morning many moons ago, I was supposed to be at a high-stakes meeting in Geneva with visiting executives, including the new CEO. They were on a whistle-stop tour of Europe and I was on the agenda to talk about my division.

But while the group was exchanging small talk over coffee and croissants in the conference room, I was just then waking up in my bed - a solid two-hour drive away. Not my finest hour. So how do you think I handled this embarrassing situation?

Here are your options:

a. *I made a quick call, apologised, threw on my best outfit, and drove like my job depended on it, or*

b. *I thought, "Well, this week's a write-off - I may as well stay home until Monday and try again next time the execs are over…"*

If you're rolling your eyes and thinking, "Of course, you chose the first option," you're right - I did. But this book is about changing your relationship with alcohol, so let's consider what usually happens when things go wrong with drinking.

Let's say you committed to Dry January, but cracked and drank half a bottle of wine on January 12th. Most people in this situation do not pick themselves up and keep going. Instead they give up for a bit, stew on their lack of willpower and reprimand themselves with a stern talking-to. Then they decide to *wait* - perhaps until February 1st or at least until the following Monday - before trying again. It's another form of all or nothing behaviour which we've come to accept as completely normal.

That stops today. The third and final component of your Off Switch is the ability to evaluate and learn from your mistakes so you *keep going*. This skill ensures you bounce back right away instead of giving up or waiting for the 'perfect' time to try again.

The Off Switch: How It Works

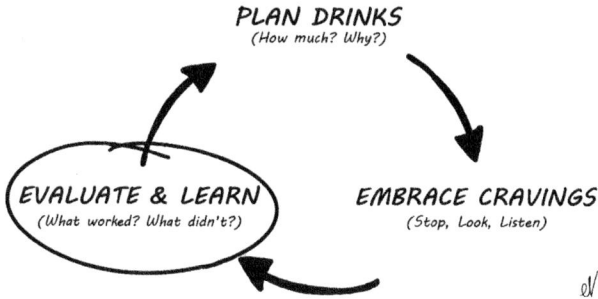

PLAN DRINKS
(How much? Why?)

EVALUATE & LEARN
(What worked? What didn't?)

EMBRACE CRAVINGS
(Stop, Look, Listen)

Actions Create Results

Take any action and you'll get a result. Take no action and you'll still get a result. It might be the outcome you want - or the complete opposite of what you intended. But either way, you'll always get a result.

If you consistently follow the process in this book, you will develop a more mindful approach to drinking and your life will change. The only way you will deviate from your goal is if you stop planning, give in to cravings, or stop looking at the trend and fail to make adjustments.

Every now and then things will go off track. You won't write a plan. You'll forget what you're supposed to do. You'll give into cravings. But none of this has to be a problem - what matters most is how you respond when things go wrong.

A Skills Shortage, That's All

We are taught from a young age to avoid failure at all costs. At school the focus is on becoming an A-grade student, never failing a test and always striving for top marks. Logically, this makes sense. Failure means not getting your desired result and brings forth negative emotions like humiliation, disappointment, embarrassment and frustration. It can stop us from taking action.

But *fear of failure* is even more insidious. Every day I talk to people who are sick and tired of drinking too much. They know they want to change, but they are so afraid of failing (again) that they end up doing nothing. This makes them feel more stuck than ever. In fact they go backwards because every time they reward a craving with a drink, they reinforce the habit they don't want, making it even harder to change.

So it's time to reframe past drinking failures as a *skills shortage* not a character trait. When learning how to do anything new, from flying a plane to baking a quiche, there will be setbacks. We understand this; it makes sense. In fact, we expect failure. We don't say, "I'm obviously one of those people who will never be able to fly a plane" or "Baking is just not in my DNA." We don't throw in the towel and give up. We figure out what went wrong and give it another go. Have you ever watched a child learn to walk? All the falling over and getting back up. It's fail, fail, fail, fail, fail, fail, fail … success. Toddlers aren't naturally 'bad' at walking - they just haven't developed the skills yet.

Adopt this attitude when transforming your relationship with alcohol. Reframe the challenge as, "I'm learning the skill of saying no and of not giving in to cravings when faced with my favourite drink." If you find this difficult, that's okay. It's a normal part of the learning process. Besides, the challenge is not the end result. It's the way *through*. It's *how* you create your new identity as a take-it-or-leave-it drinker.

Evaluate Everything

Another key part of mastering a new skill is reviewing what happened and learning from mistakes. There is no end to what you can evaluate: drink plans, your trend line, cravings, social events, nights in. By learning from your mistakes and making adjustments, you'll discover what works for you and what doesn't, allowing you to progress faster.

If you're resistant to this idea, I get it. I used to feel the same way. Evaluating may feel tedious and like a waste of time. But when I started to evaluate my actions, plans, thoughts and cravings, things began to change. I found the benefits of doing this far outweighed the effort required. Besides, it's really simple. Just ask yourself three questions:

1. What worked?
2. What didn't work?
3. What could I do differently?

Focus on identifying *at least three things* that worked before moving on to question 2. Really. At least three things. Even when you don't think there's anything positive to say. Even when you feel like you're going backwards. There are always positives, even if they are just small glimpses of success. By starting with what worked, you're training your brain to look for evidence that you are making progress, instead of listening to your old stories that it's all going wrong!

You'll probably have no trouble answering question two, but if you struggle with question 3 in identifying what you could do differently next time, stay with it. Confusion is an indulgent emotion that will keep you from taking action. Saying, "I don't know," is simply another habit your brain has got used to. If you're really struggling, challenge yourself to come up with any kind of answer. And if you really draw a blank, take a *guess*. Then try out your suggestion. Getting this right all the time is not the point. The important thing is that by being curious and asking questions, you interrupt the habit and keep moving forward. You're trying new approaches rather than following the same old routines. You're making new, powerful decisions even if your follow through doesn't yet match your aspirations.

In doing this you are also changing your relationship with yourself and with commitment. An all-or-nothing relationship with commitment doesn't serve you - "I was committed and I did it right" or "I broke my commitment, I am bad so now I may as well drink as much as I want." Instead, ask how can you extract value from the slip-up? How is it giving you insight into something you're missing?

As you answer the questions you'll see your regular patterns emerging. Be equally alert to 'one-offs' - seemingly innocent or isolated incidents 'that appear insignificant. Things like not ordering wine but always taking a few sips from your husband's glass, not minding if your glass gets topped up even though that wasn't part of the plan, or pouring yourself the remnants from a bottle to avoid waste. The correction needed to restore balance in these situations is usually very minor and easily made if you monitor the trend line. But one-off after one-off after one-off becomes a pattern, at which point the temptation to abandon your Off Switch and claim, "See! It doesn't work for me!" can be overwhelming. By paying attention you won't let things get too far out of hand.

Deep Curiosity

For those wanting to delve deeper, consider these additional evaluation questions:

- What am I feeling right now?
- What feeling am I seeking?
- How can I choose to think about what's happening?
- How can this be easy?
- What does alcohol represent to me?
- What is my desire really about?
- Why is it hard for me to say no?
- How do I feel when I'm the odd one out?

Questions and curiosity help identify which feelings are preventing you from taking action and what you need to be willing to think, feel and do in order to achieve your desired results.

Use Failure as Fuel

Evaluations might feel uncomfortable at first. Even though the first question focuses on wins, you may not relish the prospect of answering the second question, which requires picking through last night's wreckage to highlight everything that went wrong. Always approach the evaluation process with compassion, not judgment. Stay curious. For example, if you find yourself over-indulging on weekends, ask why. Do you overdo Sundays because you're dreading work on

Monday? Or because you're actually using willpower to get through the week? Conversely, if you're finding it easy to drink just two glasses of red wine at Sunday lunch, what would it take to have just one?

Being compassionate is not the same as letting yourself off the hook. It's not saying, "Okay I screwed up, whatever." On the contrary, instead of blaming yourself or believing nothing will ever change, evaluations will encourage you to take action - to develop a different hypothesis, test it and decide on your next step. Beating yourself up will just make the process even more painful and less likely you'll be willing to do any kind of evaluation in future.

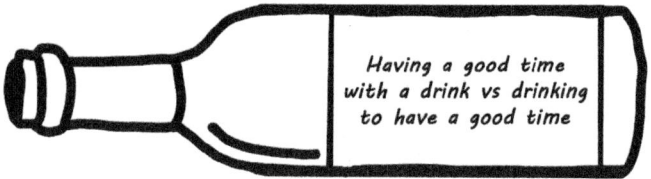

Having a good time with a drink vs drinking to have a good time

Evaluations Boost Self-Trust

The more you evaluate, the more you celebrate what works and learn from what doesn't, the more your confidence will grow. You'll feel capable. You'll see the skills you still need to learn and you'll be willing to do the work. You'll have proof that you're growing. You'll see yourself learning to drink as planned. You'll believe that cravings have no power unless you decide to act. You'll learn you can trust yourself to follow through on your decisions.

The more you learn from your evaluations, the more you'll see how you're learning to drink what you *choose for yourself,* rather than what somebody (including your past self!) says you "*should*" drink. This feels marvellous. This is when you stop seeing alcohol as the main event. You'll understand the difference between having a good time with a drink versus drinking to have a good time. You're in take-it-or-leave-it land.

There is no reason to not do evaluations. This method allows you to test what works *for you* and move forward. Do this repeatedly and evaluations will become your secret to success.

CHAPTER SEVEN

Tips

Whenever things get tough I remind myself of the tale of two frogs.

Two frogs fell into a deep bowl of cream. One was an optimistic soul, but the other took the gloomy view, "I shall drown," he cried, *"and so will you." So with a last despairing cry, he flung up his legs and said, "Goodbye." The other frog replied with a merry grin, "I can't get out, but I won't give in! I'll swim around till my strength is spent, Then will I die the more content." He swam with all his might, his splashes turning the cream into a frothy whirl. At last, he stopped and found himself perched on a block of butter. With a cheerful leap, he hopped out of the bowl!*

You've built your Off Switch and it's ready to go. You've learned how to create a drink plan you can stick to, how to embrace cravings in a way that reduces your desire and how to evaluate as you go. But perhaps you still feel a hint of doubt? Afraid you'll go back to the bad old ways? It's only natural to worry whether you'll be able to maintain this new relationship with alcohol. Friends who say, "It won't be long before you get bored and start having fun again," are unlikely to ease your concerns.

People who rely on willpower or use the traditional avoidance, distraction or resistance techniques often end up drinking again. Perhaps this has happened to you in the past? Just when you thought you were strong enough to go to the party, have a couple of drinks and call it a day, everything fell apart. In those moments, it's tempting to assume you've been right all along: that you're just someone who doesn't know how to drink normally and never will.

But this time is different from previous attempts when you relied on willpower and force. You now understand the cause of the problem and have a solution that works: a proportional control negative feedback system via your Off Switch. It is robust, reliable, stable and trustworthy. But there will still be challenging days when unexpected difficulties crop up.

You might find yourself relating to these frogs more than you'd expect. The bowl of cream? That's the challenge you're facing with alcohol. It can feel overwhelming, suffocating even. You might be tempted, like the first frog, to give up before you've even started. But I want you to channel the belief of the second frog. The one who kept swimming, who refused to give in. Because here's the thing about changing habits – it's not about making one big leap out of the bowl. It's all about the steady, sometimes tiring work of simply keeping going, no matter what!

Welcome to the chapter where we dive into a range of tips, tricks, and practical strategies aimed at boosting your confidence and providing the encouragement you need to stay motivated. Each tip is like one of those swimming strokes. On its own, it might not seem like much. You might try one and think, "This isn't working. I'm still in the cream." But remember – the frog didn't know it was churning butter. It just kept going.

That's what I'm asking of you as we dive into these strategies. Try them. Keep at them. Mix them up. You might not see results immediately, but with persistence, you'll start to feel the cream thickening around you. Then one day, perhaps sooner than you think, you'll find yourself on solid ground, looking back at the challenge you've overcome. Remember, you're not just reading tips – you're learning to swim. You're churning the struggle into the foundation for a brand new life.

Act Now

The most important advice is to act now. Start right away. Even after reading this book, which likely only took a couple of hours, you may be thinking, "Sounds good, but I'll wait until life's less hectic." You may be hesitating, waiting for the mythical 'right' time. When the summer vacation's over, when the kids are back at school, when you've moved house, when this, when that … Listen, there is no 'right' time. You've been waiting for years and where did that get you? If you feel nervous, that's okay. It's understandable. Especially if you have failed attempts behind you.

Instead of dwelling on fear, think of all the times in your life when you were nervous about something but went ahead anyway. Don't let fear stop you. Focus on what's on the other side of those nerves: freedom around alcohol. There is no perfect moment, so do yourself a favour and start right now. *Today*, not someday. Even if you have a very active social life, hang out with heavy drinkers, or have an unpredictable schedule. Just dip your toe in the water, whatever the temperature and time of year. Start with one small step then gradually progress until you realise it's not as bad as you thought. As the renowned author Doris Lessing said, "Whatever you want to do, do it now. The conditions are always impossible."

Bad Days

Successfully changing your relationship with alcohol ultimately requires motivation from within; you need to believe in the worth and value of accomplishing this above whatever effort is required.

The worst moments of this transformation are when you come face-to-face with triggers and it's just you and your cravings. This is when you may feel alone, especially if you're surrounded by people you can't confide in or who just don't get it. But whatever your real life circumstances, you are still truly alone because only you have the power to stay on your drink plan.

Remember this: if you do pour yourself a drink in that

moment, you're taking the first step to throwing out your drink plan. The next time it may not take quite as bad a day or you'll latch onto some other handy excuse and before long your Off Switch will lie abandoned and your drinking back on an upward trend. What helps in moments like this is to reflect why you got into this situation in the first place and weigh up the temporary discomfort of cravings against the permanent discomfort of never achieving your goal.

Bottomless Brunches

The alcohol version of 'all you can eat' buffets... the essential difference between this kind of drinking and normal outings is *the faster you drink, the more you get and it's all paid for so get as much as you can*. When there's a huge amount of free-flowing booze on offer it's especially important to have a plan. There may be a temptation to inflate your plan as it would be a "waste" to not drink your fill, but how would the future low-to-no-drinking version of you show up at a bottomless brunch?

The best way to deal with bottomless brunches is to treat them as if they were a 'normal' event where you would pay for every drink.

If there's booze left over, so be it; in my experience someone will always snaffle it. Even if they don't, far better to let it go to waste, shameful as that might seem in the moment, than have it go to your head and berate yourself your lack of control.

Celebrate Every Success

Celebrate each time you're aware of a craving. Celebrate each time you find yourself thinking about your drink plan. Celebrate every time you add a star to your cravings chart or every time you add a bead, button or pasta shape to your cravings jar. Each of these represents a drink you didn't have. Celebrate it all. Though not with a drink, obvs.

Do Not Seek Perfection

If you err on the side of perfectionism, it's crucial to recognise that taking imperfect action is better than taking no action at all. I'm sure you've heard this before. However if you still find this a challenging concept, let me reassure you with the habit formation process:

GETTING STARTED PHASE: Expect to falter about 80% of the time when attempting new behaviours like writing drink plans, sticking to them, or embracing cravings. Don't be discouraged; you're still succeeding 20% of the time, which is a significant improvement on before. Your main task during this phase is to *stay aware and focused.*

MOMENTUM PHASE: As you progress, you'll be practicing the new habit 40% of the time. This is substantial progress, even though you won't be writing drink plans, embracing cravings, or looking at your trend lines for even half the time. During this phase it's crucial to become your own *encourager.* Even small wins will help you to maintain forward momentum. Celebrate them.

TURNING POINT PHASE: Now the percentages flip and you're defaulting to the new habit 60% of the time. It's getting easier and things are working more often, but 40% of the time you're *still* forgetting the new behaviours. This is when resentment can peak and negative self-talk surface. You may find yourself saying things like: "Why can't I ever learn?" "What is wrong with me?" "I don't know why I can't get it

..." Focus on *not being too hard on yourself* during this phase. You may think you should be doing better by now, but that's not true. Give yourself a break. Remember that forming new neural pathways takes time, especially if you're breaking long-standing habits. You won't change a 30-year habit in three weeks.

HABIT PHASE: You're now taking the new action 80% of the time, feeling like it's working well. You'll still forget the new behaviours occasionally, but imagine how different life will be when most of the time you're planning drinks, no longer fearing social events and unbothered by old triggers. This phase is about *evaluating, learning from feedback and moving forward*. And no, there isn't a perfect phase at 100% because life isn't about being perfect. The goal is progress and consistent improvement, not flawless execution 100% of the time.

Drink Water

It will come as no surprise that drinking more water will help in this process. Before you roll your eyes and say, "That old chestnut," think about this seriously. Taking a glass of water between each alcoholic drink not only slows down consumption, but gives you space to Stop, Look and Listen to the cravings.

Staying hydrated has another advantage - it helps you distinguish between genuine alcohol cravings and simple thirst. Our brains get confused about this - so when you say, "I need a drink," you may actually need hydration. This one realisation alone has changed the lives of my clients.

The best way to make sure you're drinking enough is to carry a water bottle with you every day and aim to finish it before bedtime.

Feel Proud in the Moment

Research on habits shows that the prouder you feel about some aspect of your identity, the more motivated you'll be to continue that behaviour. So if you feel proud of actually putting your Off Switch into practice, you'll feel motivated to keep doing it. Focus on how you feel when you stick to your plan, when you refuse a drink, when you make decisions that support the new version of you. Celebrating how you're showing up in this way won't just make you more willing to keep going, it'll feel better too.

"How Will It Feel to Ignore My Drink Plan?"

This is a great question to ask if you're wavering over a craving. Think how you'll feel if you deviate from your drink plan. You've worked hard to get to this point and now it's all on the line. All that planning, craving management and progress tracking - it's all for nothing if you ignore your drink plan whenever it's inconvenient. Weigh the momentary satisfaction of giving in to a craving against the sense of accomplishment you'll experience tomorrow, knowing you've navigated a challenging situation and stayed on course.

Remember that succumbing to a craving reinforces unwanted behaviour. Ask yourself which outcome you prefer: another star on your star chart - proof that you are moving towards your goal - or the blame game the next morning.

"I Can Have It Tomorrow"

If you really want a drink, remind yourself you can still have it. Just not today.

It Gets to Be Easy

Think about the future version of you who can do this with ease and who has it all figured out. Lean into that and draw upon their wisdom. When things feel challenging, ask yourself what that version of you would do in this moment. Then go and do it.

Keep a Brag Book

Keep a 'brag book,' where you note three things you're proud of each day. This practice will help you stay focused on the positives.

Less Is More

Each time you drink less, reflect on what you gain *more* of. Is it self-esteem? Confidence? Resilience? Then ask yourself which you prefer: more alcohol or more self-esteem? More wine or more confidence? More beer or more resilience? Works every time.

Make Every First Drink Non-Alcoholic

Even if you have a solid drink plan in place, I recommend you *always* start with a non-alcoholic drink. It will quench your thirst, insert a natural pause and buy you time, especially if you're a bit too excited about your first glass of wine. You can still have your planned drinks afterward.

No Day Ones

I suggest that when you start this process you do not call it, "Day one." Even if your ultimate goal is sobriety, I strongly recommend that you do not count days sober. The Off Switch method is *not* about protecting a perfect streak of days. It's about learning to trust yourself, plan intentionally, embrace cravings and learn from mistakes to rewire your relationship with alcohol.

Similarly if you experience a setback, *do not go back to day one*. Just evaluate what happened and continue from where you left off. Aim for progress over perfection every time.

Remember Your 'Why'

You're going to all this effort for a reason. Perhaps several reasons. Make your 'why' so compelling that sticking with this process is not optional (remember: none of your reasons to date has been good enough). A great way to test your why in the moment is to ask yourself, "Why do I drink and do I like my reason?" and "Why do I want to stop and do I like my reason?" It's powerful to write these down and read them regularly. This practice will help you feel empowered, especially during tough times.

Take a Before Picture

As you reduce your drinking, changes to your physical appearance (clearer skin, shinier hair, weight loss) happen gradually and may be hard to notice day-to-day. While your trend lines show your progress, there's nothing like comparing your current appearance to how you looked when you started. Ask someone to snap a couple of pictures of you at the beginning of the process.

As you operate your Off Switch there may come times when you could do with a spot of encouragement - a sign of how far you've come. Visual proof of the progress can be a real motivator. The process may not always feel fun, but the rewards are right in front of you. Even after you've reached your ideal relationship with alcohol and your Off Switch becomes automatic, keep your 'before' picture around. Sometimes the years you spent worrying about your drinking can seem so far away that the small annoyance of planning and controlling your drinking may seem unnecessary. Whenever that occurs, pull out those pictures. Then you'll remember why you still use your Off Switch.

Think Highly of Yourself

Failure is inevitable in this process. You'll forget to write drink plans. You'll fight cravings. You'll have days when you just want to give up. Expect it all, but worry about none of it. What matters most is how you show up when you fail. Do you want to beat yourself up until you'd rather give up on your dream because you can't stand how it feels? Or do you want to support yourself compassionately through the ups and downs? That is within your control. When times feel tough, stop the negative self-talk, choose to think highly of yourself and keep going.

What matters most is how you show up when you fail

Turn Down Free Drinks

I recommend you never accept free drinks. In fact, I recommend you make that decision right now. If you find this a struggle, remember there's likely a reason the drinks are free: they probably can't sell the stuff! If you're still tempted, ask yourself if you would buy the drink with your *actual money*? If not, then of course you decline the free offer. Sticking to your plan is more important for your long-term goals and self-esteem than accepting a drink just because it's *free*, right?

Watch Your Words

Pay attention to your words. If you go around saying, "I like the taste of wine" or, "I'm never going to change," ask if it serves you to carry on repeating these stories? And if you really truly believe you like wine so much, consider how your life would change if you liked other things *more*?

You Are the Boss

Remember you decided this for yourself. You decided to cut back. You decided to read this book. You decided to want something different for yourself. So what if it feels hard sometimes? Through this process you're becoming the person who does what they say they will do. Because you are in charge. You have your own back. You are the boss.

CHAPTER EIGHT

The Miracle

It's a new miracle drug, it'll be a miracle if you can afford it

One story from my corporate days - likely shared during one of those endless team-building offsite meetings that were all the rage in the '90s - has always stuck with me.

A team of high-achieving executives had hired a consultant to *help them develop better work-life balance. He brought in a five litre glass jar and filled it with large stones. He asked the group if the jar was full. The group agreed that the jar was pretty full. But then he pulled out a bag of smaller pebbles like you would find in a fish tank, and poured them in as well. As he shook the jar, the smaller pebbles fell into the spaces between the large rocks. Again he asked, "So, is the jar full?" The group was more hesitant, now, though. So, they waited to see what he would do next. Not to disappoint, he pulled out a bag of sand and poured it into the jar as well. "Now is the jar full?" One of the sales directors in the front row, learning his game said, "No, you can still pour water into the jar." So he did. Another woman commented, "I get it. The point is that no matter how busy our schedule is, you can always cram something else in, right?"*

The consultant smiled at her and said, "Not exactly. My point is that the big items only fit into the jar at all because we put them in first. If you don't focus on the big things like spending time with your family and doing stuff that really matters to you, the little things will always seep in and take up all the space."

Changing your relationship with alcohol is like one of those big rocks in the jar. It's a significant, life-altering decision that won't fit into your life unless you *make* time and space for it. The smaller, less important tasks and habits in your life are like the pebbles and sand; they'll always find a way to fill up your time if you let them. But if you commit to tackling this big change and succeed, you'll no longer have the 'finally do something about my drinking' rock taking up space in your jar. You'll have achieved your goal, freeing up room for other more important priorities in your life.

An Evolving New Reality

The more you practice the skills in this book, the more capable you'll feel. You will learn through repetition, becoming increasingly comfortable with the process over time.

After a week or two, the worst will be behind you. You've made the decision to change your drinking habits and will have started taking action. You're writing and implementing drink plans. You're embracing cravings. You're counting cravings. Your drinking habits will start to change, but it may take some time before you notice the effects.

After the initial hump, you'll enter the main part of the process, where you'll remain until you reach your goal. Over time, you'll find that planning becomes easier. You'll grow accustomed to drinking less, to deciding ahead of time how much you're going to drink and drinking just that. You'll start to feel more neutral. With your newly developed Off Switch, you'll know you can stop when you want.

Once you begin to notice improvements in your sleep and energy levels, you'll enter the pay-off period, where the benefits outweigh any discomfort. You've successfully created a new habit and using the Off Switch will become effortless.

Fear of Reverting to Old Habits

You need no longer worry about "going back to the bad old days." Your Off Switch will continue to work *as long as you keep using it*. But if you put it away and revert to relying on your in-built feedback system to indicate when you've had enough, you will get the same result as before. Your drinking will start to creep up and before long all progress will be erased.

Don't take away the guidance your Off Switch gives you.

Imagine taking back a deaf person's hearing aids and telling them, "Sorry, you're on your own now." That would be unthinkable, right? So don't do the same with your Off Switch. It works! Just use it and get on with your life.

Causes for Confidence

Implementing your personalised Off Switch will give you many reasons to feel confident:

You're armed with knowledge and direct personal experience that tells you how your cravings work. You don't need to trust books, even this one. You've created an Off Switch, seen it work, and used it to achieve a long-term goal that many people never try or believe will work.

You've survived an unpleasant experience, tolerated the cravings and discomfort, and there's no motivation so strong that you don't want to go through it again!

You've learned that cravings have no power unless you decide to do something about them. You've also discovered that planning drinks, which initially seemed like a chore, is actually liberating.

You've stabilised your drinking at the goal you set for yourself. Permanent drinking control is now just a case of keeping the trend line flat.

You've changed your identity and are now a 'normal' drinker. It's simply who you have become. You won't want to give this up, any more than you'd want to do a shoddy job at work.

New Dreams

The original dream was for a device that would monitor our drinking and tell us when to stop. We've found a way to decide our drinks in advance that doesn't leave us sitting in the corner gnawing our fingernails in frustration. We've uncovered the link between our thoughts and feelings of desire. We've seen how embracing cravings helps us to follow through on our drink plans. Finally, we've learned how to evaluate and adapt our actions to consistently create the results we want. Taken together these components constitute the Off Switch.

Once you've mastered these skills, there's no risk of your drinking spiralling out of control. What would possess you to abandon such a simple yet effective feedback loop that you've painstakingly cultivated? A desire to drink too much again? Not likely after all the time and effort you've put into creating a relationship with alcohol that actually serves you.

With your Off Switch in place, social invitations will no longer be a source of anxiety. You'll know in advance how much you're going to drink, allowing you to fully enjoy the experience *without fear or guilt* that you might overdo it. Home alone? You won't dread boredom or use drinking as a time-filler. You'll have achieved what once seemed impossible: a take-it-or-leave-it attitude towards alcohol. Going back to excessive drinking won't even occur to you, because life will be too good to miss.

Within a few months, controlling your drinking will feel as natural as riding a bicycle and something you're no more likely to forget. It was far from easy, but hard-won skills tend to be the most enduring. But unlike a bicycle, no matter how skilled you become at managing your drinking, you will never remove the training wheels. Each day, you'll write a plan, embrace cravings (though they will diminish over time), evaluate progress, and monitor your trend line.

If I can do that,
what else am I
capable of?

Follow the process in this book and you will not only transform your relationship with alcohol, you will change your life. Your rocky relationship with alcohol is at an end. You no longer need fear going back to the bad old days. *You are now free.* Free to explore what makes you feel good and what enhances your life - whether that includes a drink or not. And soon you'll start to ask yourself: if I can do that, what else am I capable of?

You'll continue to reap the benefits of having an Off Switch. As your life changes from season to season and year to year, you won't need to worry about your drinking creeping back out of control. You'll catch and correct any unwanted changes with small adjustments. You will plan your drinking around your life instead of planning your life around drinking.

In the years to come this transformation will continue to feel like a miracle. But this isn't luck or magic. It's a miracle of your own creation and one that remains fully under your control. And that's what makes is so powerful: a lasting reminder of just how capable and amazing you are.

Appendix: The Off Switch App

The Off Switch companion app provides a simple, structured way for you to put your Off Switch into action. Download it from the App Store (iPhone/iPad) or Play Store (Android), create a profile and get started! The app follows the 3-step process in this book:

Plan

Use the 'Plan' screen to enter a *realistic* drink plan, 24 hours in advance. Remember not to set some arbitrary drinks limit that sounds good or which you think you *should* be able to stick to. Make it a plan you are *willing* to follow. Be sure to include *why* you're choosing to drink.

Embrace

Execute your plan, embracing any cravings following the Stop, Look, Listen process explained in chapter five.

Evaluate

Record actual drinks consumed and evaluate progress. You can do this by way of the calendar view or the trend line:

Calendar view

The calendar gives you an 'at a glance' view of your results:

- A green dot signifies when you drank what you planned, or less.
- A red dot indicates when you drank more than your plan.
- A black dot signifies that you created a plan but haven't yet recorded consumption.
- No dot means you didn't write a plan.

Trend line

The trend line feature is a valuable tool for monitoring progress. It smooths out daily fluctuations, helping you see progress and stay motivated.

There are two trend lines: the top one measures actual consumption over time (are you drinking more, less, the same), the bottom focuses on drink plan accuracy (how realistic are your plans). These are both equally important.

Tap either graph to activate a vertical slider, then drag it left or right to examine the trend line in detail.

The trend line notifies you of emerging problems while they're still easy to correct. What you do in these situations is what matters most. Get curious and evaluate. Does the problem lie with you planning too many drinks? Are you starting to ignore your plans? To resist cravings? Or are you allowing yourself to dream about how much you "love" alcohol?

Whatever you learn, decide what you'll do differently, write your next drink plan and keep going.

About Anna

Anna Charles is the Alcohol Freedom Coach and host of the 90 Days Later podcast. As a high-performing leader at a Fortune 500 company, Anna was far from alcohol dependent. She just thought she drank a bit too much, but found it difficult to cut back.

Anna understands when people tell her that drinking is deeply ingrained in their lives, that nothing works and they doubt they can change. She gets it when they say that AA, traditional recovery, or declaring themselves powerless around alcohol doesn't resonate. She also knows that change is absolutely possible - and that it can happen fast.

Anna offers courses and personalised one-on-one coaching, teaching a simple, doable way to achieve freedom around alcohol. If you want to take it or leave it, visit https://90dayslater.co

This is Anna's second book. Her first, a novel called *A Thin Line*, was published in 2020.

A Gift From Anna

Thank you for buying and reading this book. If you've got this far you now have the tools to go out there and make this the year you *completely* change your relationship with alcohol. For good.

I am in awe of you. Being willing to take action and create a take-it-or-leave-it relationship with alcohol is not to be taken lightly. So I want to give you a gift to help you on your way: a free cheatsheet called *8 Habits Keeping Daily Drinkers Stuck - and How to Break Free*. To get yours all you have to do is to sign up with your name and email address at: https://90dayslater.co/8habits.

I'll be cheering you on every step of the way.

Printed in Dunstable, United Kingdom